A DRUMSTICK FOR THANKSGIVING PLEASE

A WORLD WAR II FAMILY SAGA

FRANK T. WATERS III

Interior Layout by Radical Women
Front Cover designed by Frank Waters;
final cover designed by Radical Women

Published by Radical Women
PO Box 782
Granbury, TX 76048
USA
www.bylisabell.com

Paperback print ISBN: 978-1-965561-08-9
Hardcover print ISBN: 978-1-965561-10-2
eBook ISBN: 978-1-965561-09-6

For my father and Uncle Tink who along with thousands of other American flyers risked their lives regularly in the skies over Europe in those World War II years.
And to my grandfather who had the foresight to save all the family letters from that time.

Contents

PREFACE

My father and uncle rarely talked about their World War II experiences in the 1950s, 60s, and 70s when I was growing up. I think they were no different from most veterans of that war. But in the eighties, Dad took an interest in the activities of his old 339th fighter group and even attended a couple of their reunions. And in the 90s, when he was in his early seventies, he began a process of digging out, cataloging, and notating all his old World War II memorabilia. It seems the family had saved nearly every letter written back and forth during those war years, and they'd also kept documents like draft notices, orders to report, telegrams from the war department, an official record of combat missions flown, and lots of wartime pictures. When he was finished, he put everything in a large accordion file in chronological order and sectioned off by date and duty station. Collectively, it painted a complete and fascinating picture of this family with five adult children and their struggles, stresses, and losses during those war years. Theirs was a journey so similar to that of many other American families of that time, and their suffering was far from the worst. But worry and suffer they did.

In the mid-90s, a local newspaper in north-central Massachusetts did a story on Dad's memorabilia and war letters. Shortly thereafter, he was contacted by the Smithsonian, and a representative paid Dad a visit. He looked over all Dad's things and said he'd be interested in taking them and making them a part of the Smithsonian archives. He wouldn't pay Dad anything, but at least all these letters, documents, and pictures would be preserved for posterity. Dad said he wanted to think it over. A day or two later, he called me and told me of the visit and the offer.

Then, he said, "I think I'm going to do it unless you can tell me that you might one day consider using this file as a basis for a book—either fiction or non-fiction. I'm not asking you for a promise; only to tell me you'd consider it."

I told him I needed a little time before giving him an answer. A week or so later, I called him back and told him I would consider doing it. He was pleased. I think he felt his story, and that of his brother and other family members, were ones to be shared and not put away in storage. On my next visit to his home in Orange, Massachusetts. he turned his precious file over to me.

I took it home and read through every page and found many interesting and harrowing wartime stories, and I learned many new details about the Waters family during those years. But I didn't know what to do with them. I guess I was initially thinking in terms of using them as the basis for some kind of fictional account, a novel set in the World War II era. But a plot didn't come, and the accordion file sat in my reading room for several months before I finally moved it to my closet. And there it sat for nearly thirty years. I thought about my almost promise to Dad often, but time passed, and I did nothing.

As I write this, I am now seventy-five years old, and it is kind of now or never. I pulled the file out recently, exactly eighty years after that most eventful 1944 year for the Waters family, and went through it page by page again. And I found the material there both incredibly interesting and thought provoking. This was a story that begged to be told—not as the basis for a fictional tale but truthfully as it actually happened. And that is what I've done. I hope you find the Waters wartime saga as fascinating as I did.

LAURA

Dear Frank,

We received your letter last night written on the 6th, and I am going to try to answer some of it. This will bring tears to your eyes, but in the end, it may comfort you as these homey yet beautiful thoughts have comforted us.

We have seen Laura all summer so uncomfortable and growing thinner, weaker, and wearier. She knew the inevitable outcome yet still kept fighting, doing, and taking every miserable dose they suggested—whether it was something from a needle, a transfusion, or most distasteful food concentrates. And, Frank, she looked very bad too. So, living through all the summer with this shadow hanging over us all and knowing doctors could do nothing, we were reconciled when relief came to her though we grieved. John said that morning when he came home from the hospital, "Well, she is happy now if I am not."

We must not ask "why oh why?" We get all bogged down if we do. There is no answer for us to that yet. We have had wonderful and helpful letters from friends. I am sending you two; they are sad but comforting.

Our last memories of Laura are more cheerful.

1

David said the first time he saw her after she was dressed, "Why Mummy looks just as she did before she was sick." She had on a new blue suit, which she had worn only once. Very becoming. Her hair was lovely and natural; a shoulder length bouquet of sweetheart, tiny pink roses. And the boys discovered that the pillow her head was on was soft. So our last hours with her were nice to remember.

John is brave, but he has his adjustments to make each new day and the lonely nights, but he is one of those with a spiritual background that will not be defeated. Hazel wrote to him that he had been privileged to hold a beautiful flower in his hands for a few years. This privilege and his boys are great blessings. We have known a wonderful daughter and sister but have not lost her. "She is just away," and she will not grow old. We will keep our memories of her youth. Dear, we have had so many wonderful and uplifting messages from people far and near, old and young that we feel loving arms are around us all the time. I have tried to pass a little of this along to you.

We are not forgetting the skies over Europe—no not for one hour. We are thinking of and praying for our sons.

All our love to you dear,
Mother

THIS LETTER WAS WRITTEN by my grandmother, Lue Smith Waters, to her son, Frank Jr., about three weeks after the death of her oldest daughter, thirty-four-year-old Laura Waters Stearns, from acute leukemia on August 21, 1944. Laura left behind her husband, John, and two young sons aged ten and nine. Frank Jr.

was at the time a fighter pilot for the US Army Air Corps stationed in Fowlmere, England, flying combat missions over Germany and France. My grandmother, like many mothers around the world, had much to worry about during those awful World War II years with two sons and a son-in-law serving as pilots in the European theater and a precious daughter fighting and losing her battle with cancer here in the states.

For the Waters family, 1944 was a particularly eventful year.

THE OLD HOME TOWN

Orange, Massachusetts in the early 1940s was a blue-collar town of nearly six thousand people nestled around the banks of the Millers River in the north-central part of the state about seventy-five miles west of Boston. The town center, "the square," fittingly was at the confluence of North and South Main Street and East and West Main. The several four-story brick or frame buildings located there housed retail stores and offices. A beautiful stone library and the Orange Movie Theater sat a few steps away along East Main St.

On the banks of the river to the east stood Rodney Hunt Machine Company, a manufacturer of sluice gates and other water control devices. To the west sat the Minute Tapioca, a once independent now General Foods owned plant making Minute Tapioca and Minute Rice. Much of the town's workforce toiled at these successful and bustling factories or at LS Starrett Company, a manufacturer of precision measuring devices, in Athol to the east or the Erving Paper Mill in Erving to the west.

A couple of blocks away from the center along South Main St. stood Orange High School, whose outdoor athletic fields were located at the Town Park along East River St. The park was a popular place in those years with its large playground for smaller children, a bandstand for Friday night band concerts in spring and summer, and its picturesque baseball diamond with its skin infield, dugouts, and stone grandstand constructed with WPA funds in the early years of the depression. And there was even a nice grassy hill near the tennis courts, which was ideal for sledding in winter and a good vantage point for watching baseball in warmer weather.

Frank T. Waters, DDS grew up here and came back home to practice after graduating from dental school in Philadelphia. Once back, he soon met an Erving teacher, Lue Mabel Smith, who had recently arrived from New Hampshire. They dated for a bit and were married on September 23, 1903. A few years later, they built a beautiful five-bedroom colonial style home at 185 South Main St., and on May 9, 1908, welcomed their first child, a boy they named Edwin Stone. A daughter, Laura Severance, followed soon after on November 10, 1909. Five years later, on August 1, 1914, pretty little Jeannette came along. And four years after that, Frank Jr. was born on September 4, 1918. Last but not least, William Wadsworth was born on October 7, 1920. The five children grew up in a home filled with love but also discipline and educational expectations.

By 1941, as a world war threatened, the children were grown and the older ones gone. Edwin had graduated from Dartmouth and had married an Orange girl, the vivacious Marjorie Mahar, who was the daughter of the town's favorite doctor, Harold Mahar. They were living in Wakefield, Massachusetts, while he worked as a chemist for Monsanto Company in Everett.

Laura graduated from Wheaton College and took a job at G. Fox Co. in Hartford, Connecticut. There she met and married banker John Stearns and settled on Walden St. in West Hartford where they were raising their young sons, John (born 1934) and David (born 1935). Jeannette was also married to an Orange lad, Glendon "Osh" Overing, and was following him around the country where he was flying bombers in the Army Air Corps. Frank Jr. and Bill, who were students and soccer and baseball players at Wesleyan University, opted not to return to school that fall and were living at home, taking courses at Massachusetts State College, and trying to get into pilot training programs in that same Army Air Corps. War seemed inevitable.

Meanwhile, Frank Sr. was a member of the Orange School Committee and one of two dentists in town. Since he didn't drive and never owned an automobile, he walked to and from his office in the Masonic Building at 7 ½ West Main St. Each morning, regardless of the weather, he would leave his South Main St. home with his pipe clenched firmly in his jaw and make his way toward "the square" or "up street." He'd stroll by the high school and the post office with the Congregational Church across the street.

At Leavitt's grocery store and soda bar, he'd cross River St. and then the river bridge and continue past the New Home Sewing Machine Company. He'd glance to his right and see Memorial Park with its World War I peace statue and beyond the park the fire station, the train station, and the Water St. railroad crossing. Then, his eyes would come back to the peace statue of a kneeling American soldier with his arm around his young son. The inscription on its base read, "It shall not be again." But Frank knew it soon would be.

He'd continue up the hill, go over the railroad bridge and into the square. He'd see Aubuchon Hardware, Jackson's Drug Store, and the Orange Clothing Co. across the street and Woodward's Rexall Drug on his side. At the fruit and vegetable stand on the corner, he'd take a left, walk a few more steps, and come to 7 ½ West Main. His office was on the second floor. I've been told that his patients revered him, but he was largely before my time. I've also been told that this short 5'7" man with a slight build would occasionally climb into a patient's lap to gain leverage for an extraction and that his drill was powered by a wheel and foot pump. Yikes!

The older three Waters children went to Orange schools, had many friends, but were not so much athletes. The youngest two, Frank Jr. and Bill, more than made up for that. Their South Main St. neighborhood was filled with boys of similar age. Albert "Chape" Chappius was right across the street, and Earle "Brud" Witty lived three houses down over his father's funeral parlor, and the Lawson brothers, Winston ("Pint" with a soft i) and Wally, lived just behind

Frank and Bill on East Myrtle St. Henry "Ole" Olson, Kenny Burrill, Bob Harris, and Chuck Stone were also close at hand.

This gang grew up together and grew close. They were good kids, and they were very good athletes. They did occasionally get into a bit of trouble, like when they threw rotten tomatoes against the house of a boy they didn't like, or fed too many green apples to the milkman's horse, or worst of all, decided to hang a dead skunk under the river bridge. But basically they channeled their energies into soccer, basketball, and especially baseball.

In the depression years of the 30s and early 40s, baseball truly was the national pastime. Every town had a semi-pro team or two, and playing or watching baseball games was an inexpensive avocation. When Frank and Bill were in their late teens, they and this group they'd grown up with formed a team they called the Orange Peals. They played other town teams from the area with great success and soon began to broaden their horizons. Games followed against the likes of the Milton Bradley AC and Slattery's AC from Springfield and several teams from the greater Boston area. Then there were games against traveling national teams like the House of David, the Ethiopian Clowns, the Boston Colored Giants, and the Florida Colored Hoboes. The Peals were good and played before large crowds everywhere from 1937 through the 1941 season. But from 1942 to 1945, the town park diamond was largely quiet, and the grandstands were empty. The Orange Peals boys had a war to fight.

L-R
EAWIN, TINK, FRANK
circa 1936

The Waters Family circa 1925
Top - Frank Sr & Laura
Bottom - Tink, Lue, Frank Jr, Edwin, Jean

GETTING STARTED

IN THE DAYS AFTER Pearl Harbor, young Frank made an application to become a cadet in the Army Air Corps. On or about March 1, 1942, he traveled to Grenier Field in Manchester, New Hampshire where he took and passed a physical and written exam. In late March, he and his draft board received written confirmation of his pending enlistment into the air corps, and on April 20, 1942, he was sworn in at that base.

He then waited to be called to duty. He received a Termination of Furlough notice in early August, ordering him to report to Grenier Field at 8:00 AM on August 17, 1942 to begin his preliminary training as an aviation cadet. Training would be in San Antonio, Texas. The notice also instructed Pvt. Waters to bring only one civilian outfit and a small toilet articles kit as he would be completely outfitted on arrival at the Cadet Replacement Center.

Except he wasn't outfitted—at least not right away. Frank described his journey and early days thusly. "On August 17, 1942, I went to Manchester, NH, stayed overnight with other New England cadets, went to Boston the morning of August 18th and through Orange on the troop train at ninety miles an hour about 6:00 PM that evening. I waved to Father with a handkerchief—he was standing at the Water St. crossing. Arrived in San Antonio on August 20th and was sent up to tent city. No uniforms available, so spent about two weeks (through a hurricane) in a gabardine suit and civilian shoes. Had no change of clothes."

A letter he sent home dated August 31 starts, "Well, we've been having a hang of a time the last two days—a hurricane with about seventy miles an hour wind hit us and really did quite a job."

He spent much of it in a tent he shared with six other cadets. They let the center pole down, then sat on their cots under the canvas with their backs to the rain and wind. Though tents all around them were going down, theirs was OK, and he said they were "perfectly dry." Sounds like a great way to wait out a hurricane.

Finally, on September 5, Frank moved from tent city to Kelly Field and began his preflight training. And for the balance of that fall and winter, he made his way through the various stages of flight training in the San Antonio area. From October 10 through December 14, he was in primary flight school in Corsicana, Texas, and then it was basic training from 12/15/42 to 2/17/43 at Randolph Field. Finally, from 2/18/43 to 4/22/43 he was in advanced flight school at Brooks Field about six miles southeast of San Antonio.

During those many months and several stages, Frank's letters home reflected a determined, well-fed cadet who enjoyed flying. His most difficult time clearly came during primary at Corsicana. He reported that nearly 40% of his class had washed out, and he fretted over his check rides. In a letter on 11/3, he reported, "my instructor had a talk with me and said I'd have to get on the ball. Said I had the ability but wasn't showing it the way I should."

But on 11/15 he wrote, "Mr. Brooks said I am doing much better and should have little trouble with my next check ride, which is coming right up."

And on 12/9 he wrote to his folks, "This is the letter I've been waiting nine weeks to write. As far as I know, I'm going to graduate from my primary training, having passed everything and with sixty hours of flying time."

From that point on, his normal confident, cocky swagger returned at least as far as his flying went. He clearly was a little lonely and a little down to be eating Thanksgiving dinner in a mess hall and to spend Christmas at Randolph Field, but at least he got to call home both days. And on April 22, 1943, Private Waters became Lieutenant Waters as he and the rest of class 43-D were presented their wings by Mamie Eisenhower. Of course, at the time, she was just some general's wife. No one knew in a few years she'd become the first lady.

GETTING STARTED—TINK

HE SIGNED HIS LETTERS Bill, Tink, Willie, Wee Willie, Wee Wimping Willie, or sometimes just WWW. Perhaps he needed several different appellations because he wrote so many letters. I believe I've waded through approximately 2000, and those are just letters to his parents and immediate family, written between March and early December 1943 when he was in the early phases of Army Air Corps pilot training. I now know what time reveille was and what his daily schedule was like at each of the five bases where he was stationed. I feel like I have intimate knowledge of each of the "swell" fellows he roomed with or hung with during that nine-month journey. And I know for certain he was at least as obsessed with food as his brother, Frank, and made some of his army training meals sound like those found at the world's finest hotels.

Another similarity between Tink and Frank was an immediate love for flying. In a June 3 letter home, he said, "We went up for the first time today. I got in thirty-two minutes of flying time, and it was just about the most exciting and thrilling 32 minutes of my life. I just loved every single second of it, and had I had my way, I would be up there now. Most of the fellows weren't allowed to touch the controls, but my instructor evidently believes differently. I taxied the plane down to the take off place, swung it around and did everything but take it off. Then, as soon as we hit 600 feet, the instructor said you take it for a while. He put his hands up in the air and then slumped down right out of sight in his cockpit. Well, there I was with a ten-thousand-dollar airplane on my hands. What to do? I just did everything I could think of to make it go straight and to climb some more, and it actually did just that."

Clearly, Tink had aptitude and intelligence, but he never saw it that way. From the beginning of training to the end, he doubted himself and prepared himself (and his family) for the washout he felt sure to come. But it never did.

Bill was finally called to active duty in early March 1943—a full six months after Frank—and traveled by train from New England to the Army Air Corps Classification Center in Nashville, Tennessee, arriving there on the ninth. He would spend the next four weeks there getting outfitted, learning basic army discipline, and most importantly, taking a series of examinations both physical and mental to determine who would be classified as a pilot and who would be washed down to bombardier, navigator, or heaven forbid, even a regular soldier.

Our doubting Willie had this to say on March 20. "By next Thursday or Friday we should know the worst. Although there are many fellows here with much more on the ball than I have, there are also a few who are considerably dumber than I. So, here's hoping, and most of all that I get a crack at piloting."

Of course, he did, and on April 3 was shipped to Maxwell Field in Alabama for preflight training. Bill spent nearly two months at Maxwell, not flying, but learning to march, taking courses like "Maps and Charts" and "Ground Forces" and other military tactics, and doing daily sessions of physical training. There were also the one-off sessions like learning to use a gas mask and why ("I was crying like a baby in seconds when they opened the tear gas"). But though he professed to be right out straight ("I am awfully busy now, and I will be more so shortly"), he found time for a social life. He seemed to have weekend evenings off and usually had a date.

On Sunday, May 9, he wrote to his mom, "I went into town last night and had a good time. My date was really swell—very pretty, intelligent, and lots of fun. She's a sophomore at Huntington College. I have another date with her Friday."

The following Sunday he told Mom, "Next Saturday is our graduation dance. I'm going to take my little date from Huntington. I'll bet she is one of the best-looking girls there."

This was just the tip of the William Waters iceberg. By the time he left for England, he had a girl in nearly every port of call and a handful more back in Orange.

On May 31, the day before he left Maxwell for primary flight training in Camden, South Carolina, his squadron played squadron H in a softball game.

"We lost by a run," he reported, "But I earned a new nickname in so doing. They now call me 'Slugger' because of the two home runs I hit and the five runs I brought in."

He also apparently made a great catch in center field on a ball hit by a guy named Riddell who had played four years of baseball at Louisiana State. "He hit one right on the nose. I had to turn my back to the plate and dig for dear life to get to the proper spot to turn around and catch it."

That sounded a lot like a catch Willie Mays would make at the Polo Grounds in the World Series against Vic Wertz eleven years later. Wee Willie might doubt his proficiency as an aviator, but he quite clearly was confident in his ability on the baseball field.

Through June and July and early August, Tink was in South Carolina—first in Camden and then at Shaw Field. He was learning to fly. He was obsessed with it, and his letters reflected it. He was surely doing well, but worried constantly about washing out.

Here are a few of his tales from his training.

"Yesterday, my instructor told me we were going up and practice a few simple turns, some glides and climbing turns, and then perhaps a stall or two. OK, that's swell, says I. So up we go to about 5000 feet. He takes over the controls and pulls her up into a beautiful power stall while I am busy looking around at the countryside. Then, all of a sudden, he shoves the stick forward and then pulls it way back into my belly and kicks the rudder way over to the left. I looked down and there's that same dirty brown river, but this time it was spinning to beat hell and was coming right up to meet me. He pulled it out after a few times and then turns around to see how I am doing. I had a grin from ear to ear which evidently satisfied him, for he told me afterwards they had had orders that day to give us the works and eliminate the scared and sick fellows. Honestly, it is just swell, and I love every bit of it."

"I'm working on acrobatics now, and it's swell fun, but hard. Loops are easy, but snap rolls and slow rolls are tough. There is a lot of work to be done on them."

"I don't keep writing all this stuff to bother you people nor be babying myself. It's just that I want you people to know how uncertain everything is. So many fellows wash out all the time-fellows that you would never believe would-that one never knows what will happen. I just don't want you going around telling everyone I am in the Air Corps flying planes and all that when there is a chance of my not finishing up."

"We were told today that they were going to get rid of a third of our flight while we are here. Cheerful huh? Don't feel badly for me though because I won't let it get me down. However, it is very possible that little Willie will never live up to the standards set for him by Frank and Osh."

This last was written a week or so after he had scraped a wing on landing and a day after he had failed his forty-hour check ride, causing him to lament. "I am still a darn poor pilot with this B.T. I can't do a decent stall, my coordination is way off, and I hate to think of lazy eights or chandelles." He expected to be washed out at any minute.

But then they started night flying, and he quickly showed he was cool under pressure and a much better pilot than he gave himself credit for. He was flying with his squadron at 1:00 AM on Friday September 9, when suddenly his entire electrical system went out. He had no running lights, landing lights, or instrument lights, and no radio to contact the ground. Afraid the other planes might run into his plane, he decided to climb to his designated altitude and stay there until they missed him on the next radio check and realized there was a problem. Hopefully, when they did, they could provide some light for him to land.

Here's how the incident played out. "Sure enough, presently the floodlights were turned on the runway and I could see the ambulance, crash truck, and doctor's car line up beside it. Then I got a green light from the tower, meaning I could come in. I flashed my little light again (a small flashlight) to acknowledge and started in. It was a good landing too, three points with no bounce. Captain Snackenberg, our C.O., was waiting for me as I came in to the ramp to park. He was pretty darn glad to see me too, I guess. He said, 'You did just right Waters.'"

He kept doing right over the next three weeks, and on September 28, with 135 hours of flight time successfully under his belt, he graduated from basic flight training and was assigned to advanced flight training at George Field in Lawrenceville, Illinois.

Before we get to that, I am quite certain that Tink's parents were worried about him for a variety of reasons associated with this pilot's training, but I doubt if they ever worried about him getting enough to eat. That cadet liked his food and reported regularly on the meals he ate. Among my favorite contributions were these.

July 12: "I knocked off twelve griddle cakes this morning for my all time record."

And August 17: "Food actually grows better every day. Three green peppers with meatloaf, three of my sized servings of mashed potatoes, carrots, peas, bread and butter, milk, and three pieces of apple pie for dinner. It was good!"

Finally, on August 24: "Imagine my surprise as I followed Wrath into the mess hall and he called, 'Hey Tink, for Christ's sake, look at the G.D. lobsters.' There they were, a whole lobster at each place and more in the middle of the table. I was mighty hungry. There was also melted butter, lemon, and other fixings. Now Red and Swenson, being good old seashore Yankees, were just as tickled as two little boys. They figured at last they would stay with me right through an entire meal, and they did a pretty good job, too, putting away two entire lobsters apiece. But little Willie came out on top again with the better part of three safely tucked away. The three of us are sitting here burping and holding our stomachs right now, but it sure was worth it."

It is somewhat of a wonder to me that Tink could even get a plane airborne after meals like that, but I guess he did. At George Field, his group was flying AT-10 twin-engine bombers designed to prepare them to handle even bigger B-24s and B-17s when they got to combat. And the training was hours and hours of cross-country flying, instrument flying, formation and night work. As Tink said, "We won't get fancy maneuvers such as loops, snap roll, etc. here at advanced. The ship isn't built for that."

Tink turned 23 on October 7 and got lots of mail, but that's about it for his birthday. He seemed less anxious about washing out then, though he had mild concern about being made a flight instructor instead of a pilot. He was measured for his officer's uniforms, spent a week in Louisiana with his team doing high-altitude training at 40,000 feet, and hoped and prayed he would finally get a leave when this phase was done. If he did, he said he didn't want to go anywhere exotic. "This little chicken just wants to come home." And, of course, he had a lengthy list of meals he'd like his mom to make for him while he was there.

On Sunday morning, December 5, 1943, he was commissioned a 2nd lieutenant in the Army Air Corps and during the graduation ceremony received the pilot's wings he coveted. By 7:00 that evening he was on a train headed east and back to Orange for a richly deserved ten-day leave.

NEXT STEPS

WHEN LAST WE LOOKED in on young Frankie, he'd had his wings pinned on by Mamie Eisenhower, was anxious to begin flying fighter planes, but was hoping to get some leave to get back home first. It had been eight months. In typical military hurry up and wait fashion, he stayed around Brooks Field for a month before orders for leave and the next step came through. He got back to Orange and his mother's cooking from June 3, to June 13, 1943 and then reported first to Charlotte, North Carolina and a couple of weeks later to Thomasville, Georgia for training with the P-39 fighter plane.

Charlotte was great—a good town with plenty of night life, and Frank was happy with the single room he had in the BOQ (bachelor officers' quarters). While there, he was able to get over to Camden, South Carolina for a Sunday visit with his brother, Bill. And, of course, he was glad to have his basic training buddies Don Whisler, Fred Rutan, Harvey Waymire, and Elton Brownshadel with him again for this phase of training.

Thomasville was not as much fun. Maybe he was just cranky on a July 6 Tuesday, but here are a few excerpts from his letter home.

"Living conditions are lousy here at the field, and I have absolutely nothing in my room but my bed. All the windows are screened, but the mosquitos get in anyway."

"Meals are not so hot."

"Been here a week now but can't say as I like the place. The flying is fun, and the time goes fast during the day, but the nights are hell. Will be glad when these seventy days are over so I can go back to Charlotte and start living again."

With respect to the P-39, he said, "I like to fly the thing, but as yet I'm not sure if I'll be any good at it or not."

There was extensive training on combat formation flying because "pursuit planes never fly around alone but always in flight of two or four or six planes. When you are flying in tight or wing to wing, each man has to move a certain way or they may run into each other."

And another significant amount of time was spent on gunnery practice—both ground and aerial. Lastly, there was a requirement for a certain amount of night flying. While fulfilling this last, Frank "had a little trouble Wednesday night when I came in for a landing and hit the runway so hard it buckled both wings and gave me two flat tires. I was about 200' up and all set for a good landing when I turned on my wing flood light. Well, it was way out of focus and shown into my prop and blinded the hang out of me. Couldn't see a thing for a couple of seconds and instead of leveling off and putting her down easy, I flew right into the ground. Somehow I was able to keep it going straight on the runway, but with those tires being flat it wasn't too easy. This is the first time I've done any damage at all to my ship. This is not going in my record, because I wasn't at fault, so I still have a clean 201 file."

Despite this mishap, Frank was becoming a very good pilot. When the Thomasville program ended on August 31, all pilots in the class were graded excellent, above average, average, or below average for graduation day, and Frank as well as Fred Rutan and Harvey Waymire were among the eleven of fifty-one pilots in the class rated excellent.

***

At this point, Frank got another ten-day leave and reported back to Charlotte on September 13.

There he learned that he and all of his good friends were being assigned to the 97th Tactical Recon Squadron and were leaving 9/16 for Thermal, California and thirteen weeks of desert maneuvers. They would be doing "a lot of aerial and ground gunnery with plenty of formation work and some dive bombing." And they would all be flying their P-39s out there, taking three days with overnight stops at bases in Meridian, Mississippi and El Paso, Texas.

Thermal was in the desert near the Salton Sea and about eight miles from the town of Indio. There was sand everywhere, and it was very hot during the day and very cold at night when the sun went down. But the living (and training) was easy, and life was good while Frank was there. They had shorter days and weekends off and could take their planes anywhere they wanted within a 600-mile radius. So, the boys had quite a time spending weekends in Los Angeles, Hollywood, San Francisco, San Diego, and Los Vegas among other places. They'd jump in their planes and go. The only problem was that Frank was spending more money than he'd planned on. He reported spending the outrageous sum of $30 on a weekend trip to San Francisco. Imagine that.

Many of Frank's friends were married and had their wives with them. But not Don Whisler, and he and Frank became regular running mates, especially since Don had a car. But then Whisler started going steady with a nurse stationed nearby. Frank began plotting how he could get his own car (one he shared with Tink) out there from Orange.

He made a particularly touching plea in a 12/15 letter saying, "If I could get a car out here, it sure will help a lot to get me out of this lonesome mood. All of my friends are always on the go with their wives, and I'm left out in the cold. Whisler, who is about the only unmarried fellow, is going steady with a nurse from the hospital here."

Frank was like a broken record through the month of December, talking about the car and even coming up with a plan to have two guys from Revere, Massachusetts drive it out on their way back from a Christmas leave. But then, the necessary gas coupons couldn't be obtained. So Frank remained lonely.

Or did he? He never mentions a single date or girlfriend for himself in the myriad of letters he sent home. But he often talked about other guys and their dates, and I think Frank just forgot to mention some aspects of his social life.

I have no proof, but when I was about thirteen or fourteen and eavesdropping on a conversation between my parents and another couple, my mom said to my dad, "What about that barmaid you almost got engaged to when you were out in California?"

Dad was rarely speechless, but that night he was. And he looked very guilty to me. I wish I knew more.

The fun times were interrupted twice for three-week maneuvers or war games. On the first, the pilots in training were required to live in the field and sleep under the stars. But Waters, Whisler, Weymire, and Brownshadel built themselves a nice little hut out of cacti and tumbleweed and constructed a little fireplace in front and a one hole latrine in the back. There was no roof or even walls on the latrine, but Frank seemed quite proud of the whole set up, including "the pipe and funnel for #1." He even sent a picture of it home—with him sitting on it! They were assigned to either the "blue" or "red" army and flew reconnaissance missions for their assigned ground troops, engaged in dogfights with the fighter squadron assigned to the other army, and continued to perfect their aerial gunnery skills. Frank actually enjoyed the whole experience—especially the five days off that came at the conclusion of each maneuver.

He and his buddies spent the 1943 holiday season in Thermal. Dad wrote home the day before Thanksgiving.

"Tomorrow is Thanksgiving Day and how I wish that I could be back there having some of that good old turkey like we have always had. Maybe next year finds all of us together with this damn war over."

Although he didn't get back to Orange for Christmas either, he at least got to spend it with some family. Jean and Osh were then in

Tucson, and on Christmas Eve, Dad, along with Whisler and Rutan, flew down there, and the five of them had a great Christmas weekend. Jean later reported back to Orange that Rutan and Whisler were "swell fellows and what a gang they are. The three of them are a riot."

As the 1944 year was ushered in, desert training for the 97th squadron was winding down, and everyone wondered where they were headed next. Eight of the pilots didn't have to wait long to find out. On Sunday January 16, this group, including Waters, Waymire, Whisler, Rutan, and Brownshadel, was called together and told they had been selected for combat. They would report on the 23rd to Rice Field, about 100 miles up the road to the 339th Fighter Dive Bomber Group. They'd spend about a month there getting acclimated, and then they'd head to the east coast and a P.O.E. (point of embarkation).

Frank and the others drove to Rice in Whisler's car and settled in. But on the morning of January 31, disaster struck. Frank's closest friend, Don Whisler, was killed. In a letter home, Frank described the event.

"Whisler was killed this morning about 8:30 when his P-39 went into a flat spin at about 4000'. He had plenty of chance to jump out but never did. He had just dropped a bomb by diving and on pulling out of the dive must have blacked out. We believe that he was unconscious when he hit the ground, for the doors were still on and none of the switches were cut off. The plane burst into flames and "Whis" was burned some. I'm telling you about all this only because it will probably be me who goes home with his body. His home is in Garden City, Missouri."

In fact, Frank did escort the body back to Missouri. He met an undertaker at the train station in Kansas City and turned the body over and then continued on to Don's parents' house. He brought a number of pictures he'd collected of Don over the last year of training and gave these along with a set of pilot's wings to Whisler's parents. He spent two nights with the family and attended the funeral before heading back to California.

In another note to his folks, written in a train station at the start of his journey, Frank wrote, "This is something quite new for me, and I'm only hoping I can handle the situation OK."

I think he did just fine.

On March 4, 1944, the 339th fighter group left Rice Field and were trucked down to Indio, where they boarded a train for Savannah, Georgia and overseas processing (medical shots and the issuing of clothing and special equipment). Then, they proceeded to Camp Shanks, near New York City. On March 22, they were trucked to the point of embarkation and boarded the British ship Sterling Castle—a former luxury liner converted to a troop ship, carrying 5000 men across the Atlantic Ocean to England. It was time to join the battle.

Frank Jr. in his P-39 over the California desert. Picture taken by Fred Rutan 10/26/43

The hut made of cacti and tumbleweed where Waters, Whisler, Waymire and Brownshadel lived while on maneuvers (war games) in the desert early November 1943

Frank in the bathroom adjoining his tumbleweed hut enjoying a cigarette and some quiet time alone.

FUN IN THE SUN

AFTER A TEN-DAY LEAVE at home in Orange, his first leave since reporting for active duty, Bill left by train from Orange bound for Avon Park, Florida on Wednesday December 15 to become part of a B-17 bomber crew and train for combat. His first stop was New York City. He arrived there about 4:30 that afternoon and immediately looked up his father's brother, Uncle Lewis, who was surprised and pleased to see him. Lewis and Aunt Hazel took Bill to dinner and an ice show at the Biltmore Hotel. The ice show was wonderful, and the food was swell and in his letter home the next week Bill remarked, "I have no idea how much it cost, but I'd have hated to foot that bill."

The next morning, Bill was back at Penn Station and headed south again. The rest of his journey was uneventful, and he arrived in Avon Park late on Friday night. But there was nothing for him to do until at least Monday, so he and five others took off for West Palm Beach where they had a great weekend. As it turned out, there wasn't going to be much for them to do for the balance of the year. Bill didn't miss a beat. He caught up on his sleep, worked on his tan, did some fishing, and got out to Lake Wales with his buddy, Al, a couple of times to play golf. And then Bill and Al were off to West Palm again for Christmas weekend. And they cooked up an innovative plan to get some dates. In those days, all phone calls went through an operator. So, they called the central telephone office and asked to speak to a long-distance operator. When they were connected, they told the girl they were a couple of lonesome lieutenants lost in a big city and wondering if any of the operators would like a date. It worked!

Bill reported in a letter to his mother a few weeks later, "Hazel Hardin was the one that showed up as my date. She's very pretty, well built, good personality, intelligent, and about everything a guy could ask for. In fact, she's as nice a girl as I've ever had on my string."

I'm guessing Bill had a fair number of others on that string. It took a bit of time before he began to call Hazel "my girl," because initially he was also seeing a SPAR (a member of the US Coast Guard Women's Reserve) by the name of Mary Grady, who he'd met on his initial visit to West Palm. Mary was apparently smitten enough and aggressive enough to call Bill's mother, Lue, to say hello after she was transferred from Palm Beach. Bill was forced to explain who she was and to apologize to his mom for having to deal with that. And then there were the girls from Orange—Geraldine McKenna, Ardelle White, Barbara Michelbarger, and someone named Prissy, who Bill regularly reported receiving letters from.

I, of course, am happy for my uncle but feel sorry for my father, who apparently stayed back on base on fire watch most Saturday nights in California, while his buddies were off dating nurses. I'm not aware of a single girl from Orange who ever wrote him a letter. Or maybe there were a few details Frank forgot to include in his epistles home to Mom and Dad.

Right after New Year's Day, another great weekend in West Palm for Willie boy by-the-way, things got down to business in Avon Park. A total of seventy-six B-17 crews were announced over two days and immediately began training. But for some reason, Bill and about twenty or so others weren't assigned. And Bill wasn't happy about it. He was tired of sitting around, was disgusted with the army, and wished he'd be transferred to another base, which was bound to be better than this backwater town of Avon Park. But then on January 13, he was assigned to a crew—#43—as the copilot, and by the next day was already "started full blast." And like the little boy from Camp Granada, suddenly his world was right again. The pilot, Harry Pittman, was a swell guy as was every single other member of his crew. And the army, the training, and even Avon Park were good again, too.

The only thing troubling Bill now was his brother and the issue of the car they jointly owned. He'd learned through his father of Frank's desire and scheme to get the car out to California, and he didn't like the idea one bit. In three consecutive letters home, he ranted on the subject.

In the third one he said, "I think it would be unwise to let it go all the way out to California. So long as I have a share in it, it won't. It's for that very reason that I hesitated in buying it in the first place and will never own another with anyone in the future."

Thankfully, Frank was about to leave California anyway and had moved on from his harebrained scheme, saving Pop from the angst of refereeing that dispute.

For crew #43, there was much to do in a short time. They had just two months to get comfortable with their B-17 Flying Fortress and with each other. Bill quickly decided he loved the plane.

In a letter to his sister Laura, and her husband, John, he said, "What an airplane it is. Just one of those four engines has more power than the two together on our A-10s at George Field. And the instruments and gadgets in the cockpit are so many and so intricate that I'll never have to worry about counting sheep again. It's a good plane, too, and I can readily see why so few are shot down."

The crew had to attend ground school daily to thoroughly learn about those instruments and gadgets and each of their duties and responsibilities while in flight. Then there were combat tactics to understand and make second nature. After that was the flight time together. They took short and long trips during the day and night. Some were primarily training for the pilots, others for the navigator or the bombardier, and still others involving aerial gunnery for the gunners. As hoped, the crew grew closer and worked well together.

In one letter, Bill gushed, "Now that I know our crew better, I can say that I am most enthusiastic about every one of them. We really have a rare combination of men, and I wouldn't trade a single one of them." He reported that they even hung together for fishing or dinner and drinks in the evening.

But Bill still found time for more golf with Al in Lake Wales and stated he was beginning to get "really good." He had a particularly eventful weekend socially March 3-6. It seems Barbara Michelbarger from Orange wrote and invited him to her sister's wedding to a marine captain on Friday evening, March 3 in Dunedin, Florida, and Bill enthusiastically accepted, arranged to get out of ground school at noon that Friday, and pieced together bus rides via Tampa to Dunedin that would get him there on time. Except the bus to Tampa was slow and late, and he missed his connection. He would have a five-hour wait for the next one and would miss the wedding. And since Barbara and her parents were flying home on Saturday morning, he wasn't able to connect with her. But while he was stewing in the Tampa bus station about how best to salvage the weekend, he bumped into another old girlfriend from Orange, Elizabeth Gridley. Although he was harboring a grudge against her from some prewar snub, he buried the hatchet and went out for drinks and a bite to eat with her, since she, too, had a lengthy wait for a connection. The next morning, he arranged to travel another 300 miles by bus across the state of Florida to West Palm and his best girl, Hazel. It took until 11:30 that night to connect with Hazel, her sister, and Al (who was dating the sister). But then "the four of us were on our way to a most joyous weekend. Dancing, swimming, golfing, and bowling can make any soldier have a good time." What a devil!

Bill was now cross with his father, though. It was a snowy winter up north, and Bill learned his sixty-seven-year-old father had been shoveling the walks and driveway at 185 South Main that winter with Bill and Frank not around. So, Bill chastised him and told him to "hire Bobby Carlson or some other kid around the neighborhood going forward. But you are going to have to pay them well—at least $1.00." He added he was enclosing a $10 bill to cover the next ten storms.

On Wednesday, March 22, all seventy-six crews at Avon Park were notified their training was done, and it was time to go to war. They had just 24 hours to pack and be ready to go by troop train to Hunter

Field in Savannah, Georgia for "staging" and then on to a point of embarkation near New York City. Bill and the rest of crew #43 were anxious to see combat; they'd been waiting long enough. So, they were in good spirits on that Thursday, March 24 as their train pulled out, heading north. But probably about half the girls in the state of Florida were down in the dumps to see their guy Billy go.

A PLANE WITH A NAME

Frank Jr. arrived in England aboard the troop ship *Sterling Castle* and was assigned to the airfield at Fowlmere. About the same time, brand new P-51 fighter planes began to arrive there. Plane 5Q-Z was assigned to Frank with Sgt. Marion Tyson as his crew chief. After maintenance familiarization by ground crews, Frank and the other pilots checked out their new planes. Dad's first flight was on April 26, and four days later, he flew his first combat mission. He and the other pilots were proud of their new Mustangs, and most lost no time in naming them. But Dad couldn't come up with a name he liked. And despite mild pressure from "Ty" Tyson to do so, his plane was still nameless in mid-May.

After his first week of combat, Frank was granted a two-day pass, and on Saturday, May 6, he and two other pilots from the 504th took the train to London where they stayed that night and "saw the sights of the city." His letter home to his folks mentions the beauty of the country, the totality of the nightly blackouts, and a tour of St. Paul's Cathedral on Sunday morning. There was no mention of any alcohol or women involved in this Saturday night out in London for three twenty-something single guys. Maybe they were too busy touring Buckingham Palace.

Anyway, on Sunday, Dad took a train from London to Thetford and got a ride out to the airfield at Knettishall. His younger brother, Bill (aka Tink), now a copilot of a B-17 bomber had recently arrived to begin his own combat tour. The two brothers hadn't seen each other in almost a year and spent a great evening together catching up at the Officers Club. Tink was supposed to fly the next morning but didn't think he would, as it was raining then, and the shingle over the bar indicated bad weather for the morrow. So, they had a couple of drinks and caught up on their training, their travels, and their family. Frank had just had a letter from their older sister, Laura, written from a hospital in Boston where she was battling some kind of blood disorder. Tink knew nothing about it.

It was quite late when they called it a night. Tink found Frank an empty cot in another Quonset hut. They made plans to meet for breakfast and to get together again soon. But when Frank woke up the next morning, the sun was shining, and Tink had gone on his mission.

So, Frank went back to Fowlmere that Monday, May 8, and readied himself for his own mission on the 9th. He heard nothing from Tink for the remainder of that week, and the following Wednesday, the 17th, he called over to Knettishall and was told Tink did not return from his flight on the 8th. His plane had been shot down; nothing was known about the fate of the crew except that six parachutes had been seen coming out of the B-17 as it was going down. There had been a crew of ten onboard. Tink was officially MIA.

Frank was shocked, devastated, disconsolate. He couldn't bear to think that his brother might not be coming home. He needed to talk to someone who knew Tink and would understand. So, he called his brother-in-law, Osh, who headed up a bomber squadron stationed at Sudbury. Osh immediately sprang into action. He dispatched his driver to Fowlmere to retrieve Frank, and he spoke with Frank's commanding officer and arranged a pass for him. He used his connections to try and learn more about the fate of Tink's crew. In this last, he was largely unsuccessful in learning more than was already known. The plane had gone down, but five or six parachutes had been seen coming from it before it crashed. But Osh was just the listening board and crying shoulder Frank needed. The two of them talked for hours, and Frank stayed the night at Sudbury. When he returned to Fowlmere the next morning, he was in a somewhat better mental state. He believed with all his heart Tink was one of those who got out, and he resolved that he, himself, was going to fight all the harder and make those Germans pay. And he now knew exactly what he wanted as a name for his plane. And the very next day, he had "Brother Bill" painted on its side.

This picture was mailed To my mother from England in June of 1944

B-17 DOWN OVER BREMEN

THE SUN WAS SURPRISINGLY shining brightly in the skies over
Knettishall, England on the morning of Monday May 8, 1944 when
Lt. William Waters and the rest of his B-17 crew were roused from
their beds for that day's mission to Berlin. Bill may have been a little
fuzzy and tired that morning as his brother Frank had been visiting
the evening before, and the two had stayed up a little late and enjoyed
a libation or two while catching up after not seeing each other in
nearly a year. But Bill bounded from his bed, tugged on his coveralls,
and was on his way.

He settled into the copilot's seat on the right side of the cockpit.
Pilot Harry Pittman was to his left. The two, as well as the rest of the
ten-man crew, had been together for several months now, got along
wonderfully, and had become a good, well-oiled team. This would be
their fourth combat mission since arriving in England several weeks
earlier. The destination that morning was Berlin, and take off at
0613 hours was smooth. There were two groups of bombers from
the 388th squadron on this mission, and the Pittman-Waters plane
was one of eleven in the B Group. The early part of the journey
was uneventful, but as the formation crossed the Dutch-German
border, they were forced to veer northward as planes from the 2nd
Air Division cut across their combat wing. This took them very
much north of their briefed course. And at 0953 hours, Southeast
of Bremen, they were attacked by enemy aircraft.

Lt. Pittman described his recollection of the attack thusly in a letter
to Bill years later. "I remember the few seconds (though it seemed like

ages) from the time the fighters attacked until the plane blew up as follows: the fighters (12 I think) passed us on the right and turned to attack at one o'clock level. You and I shoved the left rudder all the way to the floor and gave it full right aileron, causing the plane to slip to the left. Practically all of the 20 mm shells were hitting; the right wing exploding. Fuel was streaming back and along the fuselage and burning. You stood up and put on your chute and started down the hatch. I felt the controls go limp. I flipped on the automatic pilot and stood up, hooked my chute on, and started for the hatch. Flames came up between the pilots seats. I turned around and opened the bomb bay door. The bomb bay was on fire, and I knew there was no way for me to get out. I remember saying, 'this is it.' I then realized the bombs were still in the bay. I stepped back to my seat and reached over to pull the emergency ejection lever. That's the only thing I remember 'til I came to, looking up at the sky filled with burning airplane parts. I instinctively pulled my ripcord and couldn't have been more than two hundred feet high when the chute opened."

Years later, while having a beer together at their camps on Lake Mattawa, Bill told his brother, "Frank, I don't know how I ever got out of that damn airplane. I had been shot through my left hand which was bleeding, and my body on my left side was riddled with slivers of shrapnel. Every time I crawled to the floor escape hatch, the plane which was in a spin would fling me against the inside wall. Finally, I managed to get out, pulled the ripcord, and floated down to an apple tree where I was hung up. A short distance away I could see the wreckage of my crashed bomber."

A farmer's wife who lived across the field was the first to reach Bill. She helped him free himself from his chute and cleaned and dressed his wounds a bit. But then some German soldiers came along and loaded him into a lorry with a few others from his crew. All were taken to a nearby small town and put into the local jail. Later, they were transported to prison camps. Most went directly to Stalag Luft III, but because of his injuries Bill was taken to Bremervorde XB, a "Lazaret" or hospital camp for wounded POWS. There, his hand was operated on and much of the shrapnel removed. Bill's fluency in French prompted the hospital staff to retain him for several weeks after his wounds healed to function as an interpreter among German, French, British, and American personnel at the camp. Later, he was transferred to Stalag Luft III.

In all, six of the ten-man crew of Bill's B-17 survived the attack and crash. Four died at the scene. The six survivors were prisoners of the German government until the end of the war in Europe, nearly one year from the date of the crash. Bill's family didn't know if he was dead or alive for several weeks and didn't hear from him until September 17—more than four months from the date of the crash. I can't imagine the strength, courage, and quick thinking it took for Bill to get out of that falling, spinning plane while injured. And I can't imagine the angst and agony endured by his parents and his brothers and sisters and their families during those months of uncertainty.

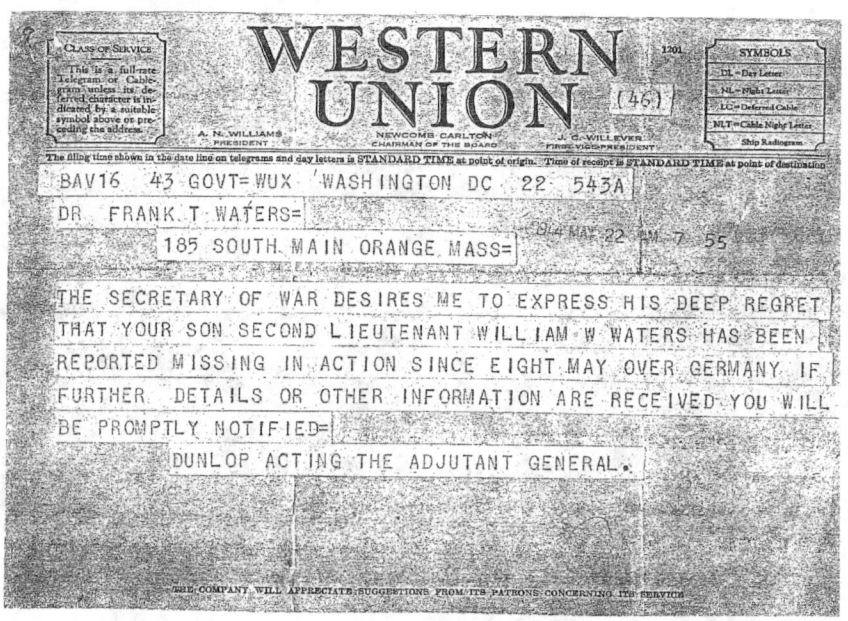

1944-England-W.W.II
Tink and some of 10 man crew under wing
of B-17 Bomber before being shot down
on 4th mission over Germany.

SETTLING IN

ONCE HE BEGAN FLYING missions and got used to the accommodations and schedule at Fowlmere, Frank Jr's life settled in to a comfortable rhythm. And in a perhaps carried-away moment, he wrote home on May 3. "Missions are lots of fun, and as far as I'm concerned, they can keep me here until the end of the war."

He lived in a Nissen Hut with several other pilots. It had a small iron coke stove in the center and doors at each end of the hut with windows and blackout curtains either side of the doors. When the stove was going, it was almost cozy inside, and it was a great benefit to be able to sleep in your "own" bed every night in war time.

The pilots averaged about four missions a week and usually had three days off. Each pilot was issued a bicycle. Frank's was #23, which he used to go back and forth to the town of Cambridge or occasionally to other nearby bases like Duxford. Frank used his days off to sleep, write letters, and play a lot of cards. Bridge and hearts were his games of choice. He wrote home often that he went into Cambridge about three nights a week but never tells us what he did there. I'm guessing a beverage or two and maybe some conversation with a female might have been a happenstance, but I guess we'll never know.

He felt a bit pampered with his treatment at Fowlmere. In another excerpt from a May 1944 letter home he said, "Boy, they really are doing everything under the sun to keep us pilots happy. As soon as we come in from a mission, we each get two ounces of good scotch. After downing this, we have hot coffee and cake or apple pie served to us while we stretch out in easy chairs in the pilots' lounge. When we don't fly, we can sleep, and we don't even have to worry about getting up at a certain time."

But they did put their life on the line every time they went up in those P-51s, and their workload and risk was about to ratchet up a notch. Frank was on a three-day pass on June 5 when his leave was suddenly canceled, and he was called back to base. As soon as he arrived, he felt tension and anticipation in the air. It was evident something big was about to happen. He observed that every plane was being painted with black and white stripes around each wing so they could be identified from above or below as American. And he learned everyone would be flying that night as the D-Day invasion commenced. His charge was to crisscross the English channel, patrolling a set altitude and providing cover and protection for the hundreds of ships below making their way to Normandy. His mission went well, and he engaged no enemy aircraft. But a fellow member of the 504th and a man Frank had been with since basic training, Elton Brownshadel, wasn't so lucky. His plane was hit by the Germans and crashed while trying to get back to base in England. Elton was killed—the second of Dad's four best buddies to lose his life in just over four months.

Obviously, D-Day was a huge success. Allied troops gained a precarious foothold in Normandy. But the hard work was just beginning. Dad flew missions on June 6, 7, 8, two on the 10th, two on the 11th, and one on the 12th before getting a few richly deserved days off. On the 7th, the day after D-Day, he was credited with taking down a German FW-190 fighter plane near Laval, France after a spirited dogfight.

Here's what he had to say about the experience in a letter home. "Have one enemy plane to my credit, and that is a FW-190, and it had a yellow nose, so it was from the same German squadron that shot down Bill. Been trying like hang to catch up with more of these babies, but every time I get myself in position on one's tail, he dives at about 550 mph for the deck and tries to make me follow him into a trap of German A.A. (anti-aircraft guns). A fellow has to think about himself a little. So I usually let the bastard go and climb out of those hot spots. Yes, I've come back quite a few times with holes in my plane, and someday, I'll be able to tell you people a couple of interesting stories. Believe that I can knock them down if they will only stay and fight, but most of them are as yellow as the day is long."

The father I knew was always a risk taker, so I was glad to read he had the sense to give up the chase and avoid the German anti-aircraft guns. But I know he was most anxious to gain revenge with the Germans for taking down his brother, so I'm guessing he found it hard to be prudent. In fact, a later letter suggests he wasn't always.

He reported, "Right now my plane is up in the hangar for repairs which is two new wings. Picked myself up a 20 mm cannon burst in the right wing, and it knocked a hole big enough to crawl through. Lucky for me that it missed my gas tanks, or it wouldn't have been so easy." That's a fact, I'd say.

He might not have worried about himself, but he was immediately concerned about the welfare of his nephews, John and David, when he read about the great Hartford, Connecticut. circus fire that occurred that summer.

In the same letter that describes the damage to his plane, he said, "Been reading about the Hartford fire in the papers the last few days. Gee, it must have been awful, and I'm not going to feel at ease until I get mail from you people telling that all is well."

Thankfully, it was. The Stearns family had enough trouble that summer.

© 339th F.G.

Fowlmere, England
Aug. 1944
Frank being debriefed
after returning from a
combat mission over
Germany.

W.W. II (1944) ..... FRANK IN HIS P-51 FIGHTER,
"BROTHER BILL" AT ABOUT 25,000' OVER GERMANY.
PICTURE TAKEN BY CREW OF CRIPPLED B-17 BOMBER
AND PRESENTED TO HIM LATER WHEN HE VISITED THEIR
SUDBURY, ENGLAND AIR BASE.
FLEW 65 MISSIONS ..... (APR. 30 - OCT. 18, 1944)

1944 FOWLMERE, ENGLAND- U.S. FIGHTER FIELD
SIX MILES SOUTH OF CAMBRIDGE WHERE RED AND
WHITE NOSE P-51S OF THE 339TH FIGHTER GROUP
WERE STATIONED. THE HANGAR WAS USED FOR
MAINTENANCE. FRANK FLEW 65 MISSIONS AND
WHEN TINK WAS SHOT DOWN IN HIS B-17 BOMBER,
HE NAMED HIS PLANE "BROTHER BILL".

1944-Fowlmere, England.-W.W.II
Frank and crew of his P-51.
L. to R.--Armorer, Frank, Assistant
Crew Chief, Crew Chief (Marion Tyson)

DID HE OR DIDN'T HE

ONE OF THE FEW war stories my father, the former Lt. Frank T. Waters Jr. did like to tell was about German Field Marshall Erwin Rommel. Anyone around the family had heard it more than a few times, for Dad always felt he was the flyer who gravely wounded Rommel in July 1944. He'd say he was in the right area on the right day, and after escorting bombers to their target in the greater Paris area, he and his wingman had been instructed to go down to the deck and look for military targets to strafe before heading back to base in England. He distinctly remembered that one of the targets he found that afternoon was a German staff car. He said he and his wingman came in low and riddled the car with shells. It careened off the road and flipped over.

The date was July 17, 1944. At the time Marshall Rommel was in charge of the German forces in France and was desperately trying to keep the Allies from Paris. The book *Rommel, The Desert Fox* by Desmond Young, a biography of Rommel's life, has this to say about that date on pages 186-87.

As he did every day, writes Captain Lang, Marshall Rommel on July 17th made a tour of the front. After visiting the 277th and 276th Infantry Divisions, on whose sectors a heavy enemy attack had been repulsed the night before, he went to the headquarters of the 2nd S.S. Armored Corps and had a conversation with Generals Bittrich and Sepp Dietrich. We had to be careful of enemy aircraft which were flying over the battlefield continually and were quickly attracted by dust on the roads.

About 4:00 PM Marshall Rommel started on the return journey from General Dietrich's headquarters. He was anxious to get back to Army Group B headquarters as quickly as possible because the enemy had broken through on another part of the front.

All along the roads we could see transport in flames: from time to time enemy bombers forced us to take second class roads. About 6:00 PM the Marshall's car was in the neighborhood of Livarot. Transport which had just been attacked was piled up along the road and strong groups of enemy dive bombers were still at work close by. That is why we turned off along a sheltered road, to join the main road again two and a half miles from Vimoutiers.

When we reached it, we saw above Livarot about eight enemy dive bombers. We learned later they had been interfering with traffic on the road to Livarot for the past two hours. Since we thought they had not seen us, we continued along the main road from Livarot to Vimoutiers. Suddenly, Sergeant Holke, our spotter, warned us that two aircraft were flying along the road in our direction. The driver, Daniel, was told to put on speed and turn off on a little side road to the right, about 300 yards ahead of us, which would give us some shelter.

Before we could reach it, the enemy aircraft, flying at great speed only a few feet above the road, came up within 500 yards of us and the first one opened fire. Marshall Rommel was looking back at this moment. The left side of the car was hit by this first burst. A cannon shell shattered Daniel's left shoulder and left arm. Marshall Rommel was wounded in the face by broken glass and received a blow on the left temple and cheekbone which caused a triple fracture of the skull and made him lose consciousness immediately. Major Neuhaus was struck on the holster of his revolver, and the force of the blow broke his pelvis.

As a result of his serious wounds, Daniel, the driver, lost control of the car. It struck the stump of a tree, skidded over to the left of the road and then turned over in a ditch on the right. Captain Lang and Sergeant Holke jumped out of the car and took shelter on the right of the road. Marshall Rommel, who, at the start of the attack, had hold of the handle of the door, was thrown out, unconscious, when the car turned over and lay stretched out on the road about twenty yards behind it. A second aircraft flew over and tried to drop bombs on those who were laying on the ground.

Immediately afterwards, Marshall Rommel was carried into shelter by Captain Lang and Sergeant Holke. He lay on the ground unconscious and covered with blood, which flowed from the many wounds on his face, particularly his left eye and mouth. It appeared that he had been struck on the left temple. Even when we had carried him to safety, he did not recover consciousness. In order to get medical help for the wounded, Captain Lang tried to find a car. It took him about three-quarters of an hour to do so. Marshall Rommel had his wounds dressed by a French doctor in a religious hospital. They were severe, and the doctor said there was little chance of saving his life.[1]

Young, 1950

Later, Rommel and Daniel were taken to an air force hospital at Bernay about fifteen miles away where Rommel was diagnosed with severe injuries to his skull—a fracture at the base, two fractures on the temple and the cheek bone destroyed, and a wound in his left eye. Daniel died that night, but Rommel hung on though still unconscious. Days later he was transferred to the hospital of Professor Esch at Vesinet near St. Germain. He was still alive on August 25 when Paris was liberated but nowhere near ready to return to military action. He died October 14, 1944, and the cause of death made public was the after effects of the strafing he suffered on July 17. It has since been revealed, however, that he more likely took cyanide pills ordered by Adolph Hitler for urging a cessation of hostilities. Ironically, his last report and attempt to bring Hitler to reason on that subject had been sent on July 15, two days before the strafing.

What about my father? Could he have been the flyer who strafed Rommel's staff car? A check of his official record of combat missions shows he flew two that day—a morning trek to Germany escorting bombers lasting three hours and twenty minutes, and a five-hour afternoon trip escorting bombers to Belfort, France.

Since Belfort is a suburb of Paris and five hours seems like more than enough time to get from Fowlmere, England to Paris and back, it is safe to say Dad was flying that day, was in the right area, and had enough flight time to do some strafing after escorting the bombers. He said he strafed a German staff car that day and watched it go off the road and flip over. Maybe the Allies got more than one German staff car that went off the road and flipped over in the suburbs of Paris that day, but I wonder. I think there is a good chance Dad was that guy who gravely wounded Field Marshall Rommel.

YOU'RE NOT FORGOTTEN

ON MAY 22, 1944, his parents received official notification from the war department via Western Union that William W. Waters had been shot down on a bombing mission over Germany and was missing in action. Days and weeks passed while they waited on pins and needles for further news. Then, one day in late June, Frank Sr. was contacted at home by several short-wave radio operators from New Jersey and Massachusetts, letting him know they heard the name William Waters of Orange, Massachusetts on a broadcast of recent additions to the list of German prisoners of war. Confirmation of that was soon obtained by Osh. Tink was alive! But where was he? In mid-July, it was learned he was being held at a POW camp near Bremervorde on the Oste River about fifty miles west of Hamburg.

Once he learned where Tink was, Frank Jr. became obsessed with buzzing that prison camp if the opportunity arose. And he didn't have to wait long. On the morning of August 5, the 339th went on an escort mission in the Hamburg area. It was a clear day with excellent visibility, and the fighters were with bombers at about 25,000 feet. Frank could see Hamburg in the distance and decided this would be the day.

He later described it. "I called my squadron leader and told him my engine was running rough and I was going to take my wingman and return to England. We made a 180-degree turn, dropped our wing tanks, and headed toward the Hamburg-Bremen area. I located the Oste River, found the city of Bremervorde, and could see a group of buildings that looked like barracks in a prison camp. Sure enough, that's what it was, and we buzzed over it just above the rooftops, pulled around and made two more passes over the place. On the last one, we finished with a victory roll then headed back toward England. All this time my wingman was with me, and it must have looked great to those guys below to see a couple of American P-51s so close. There were many buildings enclosed by a fence with guard towers at the corners. We could see guys running around waving mops, brooms, and the like in their excitement at seeing us. My only hope was that Bill was there. He couldn't help but know it was I, for the markings of my plane and perhaps even its name, "Brother Bill," could have been read as we were very low.

"On returning to Fowlmere, I told Sgt. Tyson that my plane was running fine and the reason I had aborted the mission. Even though this abortion kicked him back to zero when he had twenty-eight consecutive missions to his credit, he seemed pleased that I had found the POW camp and perhaps given hope to the prisoners there."

Alas, it was learned much later Tink was not at Bremervorde that day. He had actually been transferred some days earlier from this hospital camp to Stalag Luft III in Sagan as his wounds had been deemed sufficiently healed. I am sure he would have appreciated his brother's effort had he been there, and I am quite sure Frank's flyover did buoy the spirits of those Americans who were there.

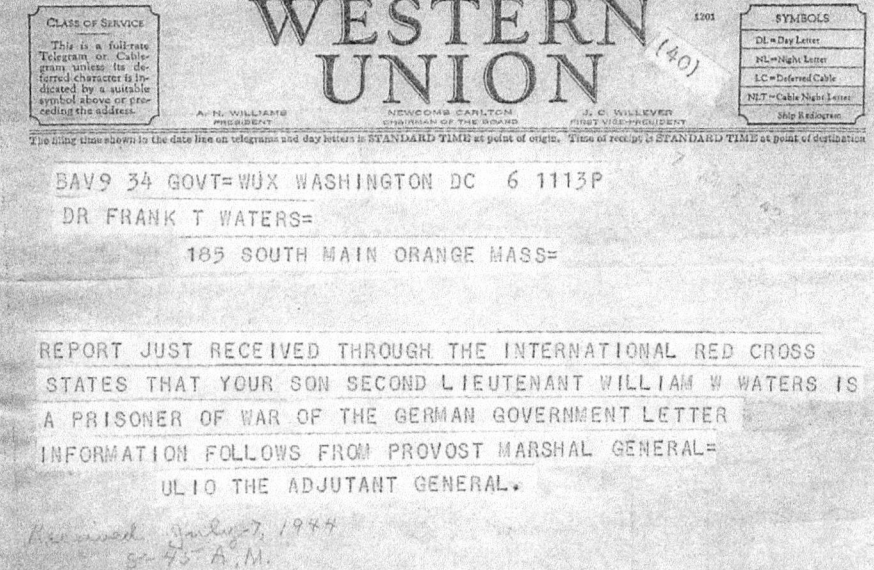

AN ELIXER FOR BATTLE FATIGUE

By EARLY AUGUST 1944, Frank Jr. had flown forty-five missions over enemy territory and was two-thirds of the way through his combat tour, but the stresses and strains of battle and the pain of loss were taking a toll. The five pilots who'd been together since basic training and had become close friends were now down to two. Don Whisler, Dad's best buddy, was the first to go—killed in a crash on January 31, 1944 in the California desert while dropping practice bombs. Then, on D-Day Elton Brownshadel had been shot down and killed while on patrol over the English Channel. And just the prior week, on July 29, Fred Rutan got in a dog fight with German fighters and knocked out two before his plane was hit, caught fire, and went down. Though he was able to bail out and thought to be OK, he had undoubtedly been captured by the Germans. Of the five amigos, only Harvey Waymire and Frank remained alive and in action.

About this time Dad wrote in a letter home, "I'm no longer the same son you last saw, because I have just had to harden my feelings to keep going. When any of my friends gets killed, we all gather at the officers club and drink. Our last drink is a toast to the one who is gone with bottoms up. We then smash our glasses on the floor. If something should happen to me I'm sure there would be a gathering of friends, a toast, and a smashing of glasses in my behalf."

After Fred Rutan went down, Harvey and Frank kept going but admitted to feeling blue. So, it was no surprise that a couple of days after Frank's August 5 buzzing of the prison camp, the doctor for the 504th, Dr. Tony Kameen, whose duties included watching out for battle fatigue, called Frank and Harvey into his office and said he thought they needed a little time off. He wrote out seven-day passes for both, handed each of them a quart of Old Granddad whiskey, and sent them off to Scotland. They took the train to Edinburgh, and this is Dad's account of their time there.

"In Edinburgh, we set ourselves up for meals at the North British Hotel. However, we had a set-to with class distinction on our first time there for dinner. Two other American pilots had joined us when we went to the main dining room. The menu listed lobster, sizzling steak, baked ham, etc. On trying to order, we were informed that they were all out of lobster and steak. We made a fuss because others were being served these beautiful meals. The head waiter, a man of about seventy, came to our table and asked if we would please step out into the lobby. He was very nice and explained that they couldn't serve us those choice meals as they were for nobility. He said he was only doing his job and did not like having to tell Americans this. He gave us a card and directed us to the Grill Room where we were to ask for Mabel. He said that we could get top meals down there.

"We went to the Grill Room and met Mabel, a very friendly lady of fifty with pretty reddish hair. She said that she liked Americans and would take care of us. Through an arrangement with the chef, she could get us the best of meals served family style. We were not to tip her until the end of the week. Well, during the ensuing week we sat at a reserved table enjoying great meals of steak, ham, pot roast, chicken, etc. She even made a reservation for a bus trip to a little harbor town for us to have lobster at the Inn there.

"Mabel also organized a tour of Edinburgh Castle, provided girl escorts and sent us to a photographer to have our picture taken in kilts. On our final night at dinner, we were served roast turkey, and at each place was a sprig of Scottish heather, which she said would bring us good luck. The chef came out of the kitchen and wished us well. Mabel, with tears in her eyes, put her hands on her hips and said, 'If you have enjoyed the meals and I have been of good service, you may give me a gratuity now.' She kissed us all goodbye and went through the door into the kitchen. We did not see her again.

"Needless to say, we left a very good tip for Mabel and the chef. We took the train and rode back to Cambridge, getting to Fowlmere about 9:30 the next morning. We later found Mabel had written our mothers about our stay in Scotland.

"During my remaining missions and for many years after, I carried that sprig of heather in my wallet."

Now, I don't want to sully Dad's wholesome tale, but I have found most of his letters and accounts from the time to be very much G-rated. And I do think I knew him pretty well. I find myself each time I read this account wanting to know a bit more about these "girl escorts" Mabel provided for them. But I find no mention here of a story I heard Dad tell from time to time about his week in Scotland. It seems Dad borrowed a Kodak camera from a buddy to take on his trip. But sometime during the week, after a fair number of cocktails, he fell asleep (passed out?) in an Edinburgh park. And when he awoke, the camera was gone. I guess his conversation with the camera's owner when he got back was not an easy one.

But Harvey and Frank had a "swell" time to use the vernacular of the day. And they were definitely rejuvenated and ready to resume flying and complete their tours. I remember seeing that sprig of heather Mabel gave him still in Dad's wallet when I was well into my teens. It clearly brought him the promised good luck.

Frank Jr. in his Kilt

LAURA'S BATTLE

THE WINTER OF 1943-44 was one of the snowiest of the first half of the 20th century in much of New England, but as February turned to March, signs of spring abounded, and there was optimism in the air. On the war front, the Germans had retreated from Leningrad, and the Red Army was pushing toward the Balkans. In Italy, the Allies had gained a foothold and were slowly moving toward Rome. And in the north, British and American bombers were targeting Berlin and industrial targets all over Germany while plans were underway for an Allied invasion of the European mainland.

In West Hartford, Connecticut, Laura and John Stearns were enjoying their Walden Street home and their young sons, John, then nine and David, eight. They were close with their families on both sides and had a wonderful circle of friends and neighbors. Laura worried about her two younger brothers, Frank and Bill, and her brother-in-law, Osh. All three were Army Air Corps pilots, and all were embarking for England and a combat tour that spring. Basically, she was as happy and as content with her life as one could be with her country at war.

But near the end of March, Laura found she was tiring easily, lacked her usual energy, and was experiencing flu-like symptoms, including a fever. When the symptoms persisted, and she began to lose weight, John decided it was time to see a doctor. Initially, anemia was suspected, so she found her way to a hematologist, Dr. Root, at Hartford Hospital. A series of blood tests suggested a more ominous diagnosis—acute leukemia.

Dr. Root consulted doctors in Boston, and Dr. George Minot, a Nobel prize winning physician there, agreed to take on Laura's case. Dr. Root, himself, drove Laura to Boston on April 27, and she was admitted to the Thorndike Medical Center, the foremost facility for blood research in the United States. A battery of blood tests followed over the next several days before the acute leukemia diagnosis was confirmed.

In a letter to Frank, written Sunday, April 30, Laura said, "I am a little afraid it is not completely curable, and I may have to fight it more or less the rest of my life." She added, "Not sure how long I'll be here—it depends some on what they are able to do for me."

In the end, they decided to experiment with the new wonder drug penicillin. Dr. Minot used his influence to obtain $5,000 worth of the drug and prescribed a strong daily dosage in hopes it might prove as surprisingly effective in eradicating, or at least controlling, this deadly disease as it had with various viruses. Alas, the experiment proved futile, and by mid-May Laura returned home to be treated locally with blood transfusions as needed to replace the destroyed red blood corpuscles and a strict protein-rich diet.

But the family also left no stone unturned. As Frank's cousin, Bill, told him in an August letter, "Meanwhile, we were investigating all other possibilities. We contacted the president of the American Medical Association (a friend of my father), the National Research Council, the Boston and Harvard research laboratories, the New York Hospital, Cornell Medical, the Hahnemann Hospital in Philadelphia, the Mayo Clinic, the Columbia University Medical Center, and many other outstanding institutions. We checked with scientific and medical authorities and located the men most interested in blood research. Several other people with the disease were found, and their symptoms and treatment compared. Invariably, we received prompt and courteous replies, but every authority confessed that little was known of the malady. They have still been unable to discover a cause, a germ, or a cure."

While Laura and John were in Boston, her younger sister, Jeannette, who was now back living in Orange while her husband Osh was at war, stayed with the boys on Walden St. and got them off to school, made their meals, and cared for the house. They decided she would stay on, even after Laura and John returned, to allow them to focus on restoring Laura's health.

Through the latter part of May and the month of June, Laura was at home save for trips to Hartford Hospital for transfusions as necessary. She was comfortable and happy and spent as much time as she could with Johnny and David. She also kept up with letter writing to her younger brothers and organizing "care" packages of cigarettes, cookies, toiletries, etc. to be sent their direction. When school got out for the year, the boys were able to spend time in Orange with their grandparents or at Lake Sunapee in New Hampshire with their uncle and aunt, Gordon and Margaret Stearns. Usually, one of the boys would be home with his Mom and Dad and Aunt Jean while the other was away vacationing.

As June wore on, Laura's transfusions became more frequent, and they were an awful ordeal. She was given a strong sedative before the process, which often took five hours or so to complete. And the doctors readied a calcium-gluconate veinous shot in case she sprang a violent chill, which she often did. They'd have to wait for the chill to subside before continuing. A full dose of one quart of red cells was the goal. And if she was able to take it all, she was rewarded with several days of buoyed spirits and increased energy. Through it all, she remained optimistic, courageous, and always pleasant with her sense of humor intact.

Then came July. In a letter to Frank, written in two parts on July 28 and August 1, Laura had this to say. "I have been quite miserable all this month—in bed most of the time with a fever and in the hospital three times. I have had a little hard luck with transfusions the past few times—reactions so I couldn't take the blood and twice had to go home without enough." But she went on to say that this time they were successful after finding a way to filter the blood differently. And she concluded, "I feel they have put me over the top this time, for my appetite is picking up and my strength is returning."

She admitted, "They found my protein content very low—thus the lack of strength and high fever. So, I am taking a quart of horrid tasting tomato bouillon formula each day, which has in it a protein powder—dextri-maltose. Am also attempting to drink two quarts of milk a day—about an impossibility for me because I hate it so, but I know I have to and find that already this stuff has picked me up. No doubt about it."

In the August portion of her letter Laura gushed over a visit from her older brother, Edwin, his wife, Margie, and their three-month-old daughter, Sally. "She is just the dearest, prettiest baby girl I about have ever seen. She spent most of her wakeful hours in or on my bed with me."

She went on to tell Frankie that she "will never give up" and warned him to be careful about these "buzzing" jobs. She then signed off with, "Lots of love from all of us—Laura."

It was the last letter Frank would get from his oldest sister.

In the early days of August, the Waters and Stearns families circled the wagons. Relatives from near and far came for a final visit. Johnny and David were returned home from Orange and Sunapee. On the afternoon of August 20, Laura's sons spent some time with their mom in her hospital room, and then her parents, Frank and Lue, did the same.

After those visits, Laura said weakly, "My job is done; I want to get some sleep now."

She went to sleep and didn't wake up again. She died at 3:00 AM on August 21, 1944, with her husband, John, at her bedside. She was just thirty-four years old.

Laura in her backyard before she became seriously ill.

UNSUNG HEROES

THE BRAVE MEN AND women who fought in World War II are rightly called America's greatest generation. As I read the letters from my father and my uncles, Tink and Osh, from those war years, my affirmation of that appellate only grows. The sacrifices they made; the hardships they endured; the risks they took; and the losses they sustained uncomplainingly that our great nation might remain free have earned both my profound thanks and my unwavering admiration.

But as I've read the letters and come to know the saga of the Waters family through the decade of the 1940s, and especially the awful 1944 year, I have also come to appreciate tremendously the burdens shouldered and the incredible strength and resolve shown by their parents (my grandparents), Frank and Lue Waters as well.

Like all parents, they were bursting with love for their five children, and they wanted desperately to protect them from harm, hardship, and loss. But they knew you can't always do that, and when adversity came, it was up to them to provide strength, support, guidance, and plenty of love to keep the family moving forward. The adversity the Waters family faced in 1944 was significant.

In February of '44, Frank and Lue dealt with the news that sons, Frank Jr. and Bill, and son-in-law, Osh, were all headed to England to join the fray against Germany. Then late that month, Frank's dear Aunt Mary, who was well into her eighties and staying with them at 185 South Main, slipped on the back stairs, fell, and broke her hip.

She was taken to Gardner Hospital for treatment but didn't respond well.

In late March, while Aunt Mary declined, Frank and Lue learned that their oldest daughter, Laura, wasn't feeling well. Before they had time to dwell on that, on March 31, Frank's younger brother, Lewis, only fifty-six, had a sudden heart attack and died at his White Plains, New York home. The brothers and their families were close, and everyone was devastated. A second funeral (after one in New York) and the burial were in Orange, and Frank and Lue opened their home to his widow, Hazel, and her children, Sally and Bill, and comforted them as well as their own children.

In April, Aunt Mary died about the same time as Laura was tentatively diagnosed with acute leukemia—a disease believed incurable. Meanwhile, Frank Jr., Bill, and Osh all arrived in England and began flying combat missions, giving them something else to worry about.

Early May brought a bit of good news as the oldest child, Edwin, and wife, Margie, welcomed their first child on the 7th—a beautiful little girl they named Sally. That good news was tempered by confirmation in Boston of Laura's leukemia diagnosis.

Then on May 22, Frank and Lue received a Western Union telegram stating their youngest son was missing in action, his B-17 bomber having been shot down on May 8 near Bremen, Germany. It would be several more weeks before news was received that he was alive though somewhat injured and a prisoner of the Germans.

June and July saw Frank and Lue with help from their daughter, Jean, and the Stearns family overseeing the care of Laura, her Walden St. home, and especially her young sons, John and David. Lue in particular was sensitive to the state of those boys, for she lost her mother when she was just twelve. Her mother died at thirty-four—the same age as Laura. Since Lue's father had been unwilling or unable to care for Lue and her four younger siblings, they had been farmed out to people in the Salisbury, New Hampshire area. Lue went to live with Hattie Watson who ran a boarding house in Warner, New Hampshire. Hattie was a kind lady (Lue called her Aunt Hattie), but there was work to be done. So, Lue cleaned the boarding house and helped with meal preparation—even killing and cleaning chickens. Because of her experience, Lue was determined to nurture and coddle John and David and make sure they knew there were always many loving arms around them.

In August, they buried their beloved Laura, wondered and worried about the health and well-being of Bill in the hands of the Germans, and fretted over Frank Jr.'s mental health and tales of dogfights with German fighters. But through it all, these two sixty-something older folks maintained a heavy workload while providing support and comfort to those around them. Lue wrote weekly letters to all her boys overseas. Frank tracked down items those boys asked for—airmail stamps, a new fountain pen, a flashlight, a padlock for a foot locker, and banked the money the boys sent home. And together they put together regular "care" packages of food, candy, and cigarettes as well as new underwear, wool socks for winter, and a deck of playing cards.

On Labor Day weekend they entertained Edwin, Margie, and baby Sally as well as John Stearns and his two motherless sons. And they made sure everyone, especially those two little boys, had an end of summer weekend as pleasant as possible. When Frank Jr. got home from his tour in mid-November, Lue had the apple pie with Vermont cheddar he'd requested ready and waiting.

Honestly, at their age, with all the angst they endured, I do not know how they kept moving forward, doing what had to be done while always providing unwavering support and comfort to their entire extended family.

They really are unsung heroes.

COUNTING THE HOURS 'TIL HOME

ONCE BACK FROM SCOTLAND, Frank Jr. caught up on the mail from home, which included a troubling letter from his sister, Laura, written in part from Hartford Hospital, describing the transfusions she needed with increasing frequency and assuring him she would never give up. Another letter from his parents used the word "leukemia" for the first time, and Frank asked Dr. Kameen about the disease. He learned how seriously ill his oldest sister was, so he wasn't caught completely unaware a couple of weeks later when he received a letter from his cousin, Bill, who was in West Hartford helping out, telling him some details of Laura's battle over the last few months and of her passing on August 21, 1944.

In part, that letter read:

"All of us had known from the beginning that Laura was struggling against heavy odds. It was impossible to replace the blood as fast as it was destroyed. And no patient had ever recovered from the disease, so we could not hope for immunization.

"Things moved rapidly this past week. Laura was gay as always, but very weak. The boys came back from Orange and Sunapee, and the relatives were asked to come. David and John went to see her, as did your parents. And yesterday, at 3:00 AM, she passed away quietly in her sleep. It was not a happy conclusion to her long illness, but we all knew it was the only possible one. And I think no one who saw her would have wished her to continue a losing fight.

"John has chosen a lovely lot, two blocks from the house here. It is just below the crest of a hill, by a winding road. All around are trees and hills. Laura will go there tomorrow."

Frank Jr. was understandably devastated. He was all alone thousands of miles from home, and in the space of a few short months lost his oldest sister, agonized over the fate and whereabouts of his younger brother and best friend who had been shot down and injured and now languished in a German prison camp, lost three of his four best pilot buddies to the war, and had not been home for the passing of an uncle and a favorite great aunt.

On September 6, he wrote to his parents that he had been going crazy waiting for a letter from "you people" after getting Cousin Bill's notification about Laura.

He went on to say, "After reading the letter, I put it in my pocket and went for a walk where I could cry and think by myself. Feel much better now and know that I can take the whole thing. Going to try all the harder to finish up and get home. Have about 80 hours to go."

This letter arrived in Orange on September 10 and prompted his mother to immediately sit down and write back to him the letter that appears in the first chapter of this book. One other note—the 80 hours Frank referred to are the remaining combat hours he must attain to complete his tour and get home. His countdown was mentioned in nearly every one of his letters going forward.

Thankfully, Frank had a couple of social outings about that time to take his mind off his misery. On September 2, two days before his birthday, Frank and Harvey Waymire biked over to Duxford to see Bing Crosby in concert. A week later, he got a phone call from Johnny Roche saying he was with Stanley "Bijah" Hinds over at Duxford and Bijah was going to play ball there. John and Bijah were friends from Orange, and Frank and Bijah were teammates on the Orange Peals baseball team in more peaceful times. Bijah was, in fact, the ace pitcher on that team and good enough to play for this army team and after the war to play minor league ball for the Philadelphia Phillies organization.

Frank reported that he immediately jumped on his bike and rode over to Duxford in time to see Bijah pitch a one hitter. He also said both of those guys looked "swell," and it was really nice to spend time with someone from home. He also reported he was down to 75 hours of flying time to go. I'm sure this was a pick-me-up he really needed.

Also about that time, Frank Jr. was awarded the Distinguished Flying Cross. The citation read, "For extraordinary achievement and heroism in aerial combat and the destruction of one enemy airplane over enemy occupied Continental Europe. The skillful and zealous manner in which Lt. Waters has sought out the enemy and destroyed him, his devotion to duty and courage under all conditions serve as an inspiration to his fellow flyers. His actions on all these occasions reflect the highest credit upon himself and the Armed Forces of the United States."

A letter he sent home mid-month contained this interesting excerpt. "I don't dare drink much coffee before going on a mission, because when a pilot in a P-51 has to go—there just ain't no place to find relief. Besides sitting on my parachute in a very low, tight seat, I have three pairs of pants on (underwear, regular pants, and "zoot suit" coveralls) plus four tight straps going down between my legs from the parachute and Mae West and the very tight four inch safety belt. All of this plus wearing my leather jacket and oxygen mask with goggles makes the normal operation impossible. More than once we come back with wet pants. Nobody takes pictures of pilots returning from long missions."

This made complete sense to me, but I'm not sure why he felt the need to write to his mother about it.

Anyway, because the Air Corps reduced the combat hour requirement from 285 to 270, Frank was down to just 24 combat hours according to his September 26 letter, and he was clearly thinking about getting home to his mother's cooking. He sent a list of things he'd like to eat when he got there, including bacon and eggs, toast, and coffee for breakfast; warm blueberry pie and warm apple pie with good Vermont cheese; a pot roast dinner "with some of your beautiful oven brown potatoes;" and milk with every meal 'cuz he hadn't had any for seven months except in Scotland. He also requested clean sheets once a week. He obviously was planning for his mother to wait on him hand and foot.

On a more ominous note, he reported getting hit by flak and bullets (his plane not him) and wondering if he'd make it back to England. "But Brother Bill has been good to me, and we made it." Those last twenty-four hours couldn't go fast enough for Frank or his parents, worrying at home.

His letter on October 5 reported that he'd made a miscalculation in his prior letter, and he still had twenty-three hours to go.

On October 7, he said, "Flew yesterday and got five hours. Yesterday I went to Berlin and today it was Leipzig. Now have only twelve hours and a half left to go and can easily do it in three missions."

October 15, Frank reported, "Well, I have exactly four hours and fifteen minutes left to go. Tomorrow and the next day are my days off so I won't be flying."

Then, on Wednesday night, October 18, 1944 he wrote this short note:

Somewhere in England —

Wed. night
Oct. 18, 1944

Dear Folks,

Today I flew my last mission and have now finished my present Tour of combat duty. Ought To be home sometime within a months Time — — I hope.

Love,

Frank Jr.

P.S. A drum stick is requested for my first helping Thanksgiving dinner.

My last mission — — Oct. 18, 1944
Escort Bombers — Kassel, Germany 4 Hrs 20 Min
Total Missions 65   Total Combat Time 270:05.

On October 30, 1944, after checking out at Fowlmere Airfield, Frank left from Cambridge by train for Stone Air Base in Wales. Stone was an Army Air Force Replacement Depot and point of embarkation for personnel returning to the states. Some returned by air while others were trucked to Liverpool to go by ship.

Frank was stuck at Stone for over two weeks because his transfer papers were misplaced. He spent his time eating, sleeping, and going to the movies. On the afternoon of November 14, while sitting in the movies, his name came over the PA system to report to headquarters. There he learned he would be flying out from Valley Air Field that evening on a big old C-54 cargo plane which had bucket seats along the sides and freight and cargo in the center. He left Valley at 7:30 PM on the evening of November 14, and after stops in the Azores and Bermuda, finally arrived at Mitchell Field near New York City at 10:30 PM on the 15th. He and the other returnees were bussed to Fort Totten on Long Island where they spent the night and got their orders the next morning. Frank would have a twenty-one-day leave before reporting to Atlantic City on December 9.

In the early afternoon, Frank went into New York City and to Grand Central Station where he found he could get a train that would get him to Springfield, Massachusetts by 9:00 that evening. He called his father, arranged to be picked up there, and set off. When he pulled into the train station on time, his father, along with family friends, Henry and Harry Anderson (who did the driving), were waiting on the platform. There were many hugs and tears in everyone's eyes. And Frank wished his father a Happy Birthday. Getting home on his Dad's birthday made everything a little more special.

They arrived at 185 South Main St. about 10:15 PM, and his mother had a warm apple pie with Vermont cheddar cheese waiting. Frank and his parents stayed up for hours talking, and his father kept saying it was the best birthday he'd ever had.

When they finally called it a night, Frank Jr. thought his own bed felt awfully good. He slept till noon the next day, and yes, a few days later on Thanksgiving, he did get that drumstick he'd been looking forward to.

LIFE AS A POW

Lt. William W. Waters was shot down on May 8, 1944 over Bremen, Germany. After parachuting to earth, he was immediately captured by the German military. Because he had been shot in his left hand and had shrapnel wounds on his left side, he was initially sent to Bremervorde XB, a hospital camp, for surgery and rehabilitation. Some two months later, with his wounds healed, he was transferred to Stalag Luft III, a prisoner of war compound in Sagan, Germany run by the German Air Force, the Luftwaffe, and used almost exclusively for captured British and American flyers. It was the camp where the "great escape" occurred a few months earlier (March '44).

Stalag Luft III was huge, consisting of five separate compounds which housed a total of nearly 11,000 prisoners at its wartime peak. Bill was assigned to the South Compound where most captured American officers were kept eight to a room. Relatively speaking, the prisoners were treated well and in accordance with the Geneva Convention. Oh, they were interviewed (interrogated?) on arrival, but there is no indication of torture or physical abuse. Rather, a psychological approach was used. The interviewers spoke perfect English and knew much about each prisoner they interviewed—their unit, commanding officer, home town, when and where they'd been on leave, etc.—and tried to make friends in hopes of gleaning useful military information. But name, rank, and serial number were all they usually got. The biggest challenges for the prisoners were dealing with meager rations, cold and drafty bunkhouses, the irregular delivery of Red Cross food parcels, and boredom.

Let's talk about the boredom first. Because the Geneva Convention said officers couldn't be made to work, there was little required of the Luft III prisoners. Twice each day, they had to muster for appel or roll call for the Germans to take count and make sure no one had escaped. Other than that, their day was their own.

In a late June letter to his parents (which they didn't receive until fall) Bill said, "I'm afraid you won't know me when I get home. All I seem to do around here is eat, sleep, read, and write letters. Consequently, I am rapidly growing fat and lazy. And the books are nothing but the best of literature, too, so I may have developed a little culture when you see me."

In another he said, "There isn't much to write as life doesn't vary much from day to day."

And in a third, he announced that he would take a nap when he finished the letter, then added, "The reason for the nap is because of lack of something to do rather than tiredness."

In one more he wrote, "I have nothing to do in the daytime but cater to my own whims and needs. Mostly I read and lie in the sun—a very lazy existence."

But the Red Cross got them a movie to watch every month or two; they could play soccer or volleyball or ice hockey in winter occasionally in the yard; and there was a portable victrola which each room got to use one hour each week.

Bill reported, "The songs are pretty old, but you can imagine how good they sound to us all the same."

It's hard to believe Bill got very fat with what they had to eat. I've attached to this chapter a listing of the contents of a weekly Red Cross food parcel along with the weekly ration provided by the Germans. Basically, that was just a crusty piece of bread and a watery broth or soup each day. And Bill or one of his roommates once found a horse's tooth in a dish of his. But they found ways to make do and even produce pies and cakes (using pulverized crackers, cocoa, margarine, sugar, water, and baking powder) and pancakes. Jelly or toothpaste were used as frosting for cakes and toppings for pancakes. Each prisoner got to try his hand as a cook. Bill's room used a four-week rotation, and each week, two of the eight roommates did the cooking and housework. Bill enjoyed his weeks on duty in part because it gave him something to do, but also because of the challenges of making palatable meals with minimal and repetitive ingredients. Bill raved about his spam loaf or especially the meatloaf supper he made from "some meat the Germans gave us," which he served with a few carrots and radishes from their garden and German potatoes.

He concluded "There will be many a helpful husband come out of this experience in a prison camp."

Preparing for winter in their drafty bunkhouse became a fall avocation. Bill reported in one letter that he and others had been pulling stumps from the yard and cutting them up for fuel for the woodstove in their barracks. Everyone asked for wool socks to be sent from home, while some prisoners learned to knit theirs. Because the German-issued ersatz blankets offered little warmth, many prisoners sewed two together with layers of newspaper between them for a filler or lining. Bill wisely requested a stocking cap be sent in the next package from home.

The Germans were good about providing prisoners with the opportunity to write a postcard each week and a one-page letter almost as frequently. And Bill always took advantage of that opportunity, though he expressed some frustration there wasn't much to write about, in part because of restrictions on what he can talk about and in part because for four full months he received no correspondence and didn't know what was happening at home.

I was amazed at how positive and upbeat every one of his letters was. He always suggested he was healthy, well fed, and as happy as one could be under the circumstances.

"Don't worry about me," he said regularly.

But he worried about them and was always concerned about his parents and his relatives, old and young. He wanted to make darn sure his father has had the house painted. I have attached two postcards and a one-page letter he wrote from camp. The letter is particularly poignant since he was reacting to news of his sister's death, which he had just learned about.

Bill celebrated his twenty-fourth birthday at Stalag Luft III on October 7, 1944.

Here is what he said about it in a letter written October 10. "It wasn't possible to write to you on my birthday as the mail forms for this month hadn't been issued at that time. Nonetheless, I did have a birthday just as I have for the past twenty-four years. It was a little different from my previous ones I must admit. Perhaps my next one will be more to my liking."

I hope his roommates at least baked him a pulverized cracker birthday cake and served something other than spam for dinner.

Bill was also there for Christmas, and he put a positive spin on that too.

"Xmas has come and gone," he said in a letter dated December 28. "Everyone here has had far better ones at home, but ours this year was certainly a good one. Xmas parcels from the states came in time to be used. They were wonderful. I'm smoking a pipe now that came in one of them. The food was the outstanding feature. Here's our dinner for that day. We prepared it all and used many unorthodox means and methods to get the final results, but they sure were good. We had turkey, dressing, boiled rice with gravy, carrots, plum pudding with good sauce, assorted nuts and hard candies, and coffee." Simple pleasures for sure. And he went on to say, "All this makes me repeat to you what a tremendous debt all of us in here owe to the American Red Cross. They have served us faithfully and constantly with priceless goods."

Bill was a prisoner at Luft III from his July 1944 arrival until January 1945 when he and all the others in South Compound were moved abruptly. And that is a story for the next chapter.

FOOD PARCELS

ONE PER WEEK PER MAN

RED  CROSS

BRITISH			AMERICAN			CANADIAN		
Condensed Milk	1	can	Powdered Milk-16oz.	1	can	Powdered Milk	1	can
Meat Roll	1	can	Spam	1	can	Spam	1	can
Meat & Vegetable	1	can	Corned Beef	1	can	Corned Beef	1	can
Vegetable or Bacon	1	can	Liver Paste	1	can	Salmon	1	can
Sardines	1	can	Salmon	1	can	Cheese-8 Oz.	1	can
Cheese-4 oz.	1	can	Cheese	1	can	Butter-16 oz.	1	can
Margarine or Butter	1	8oz.	Margarine-16 oz.	1	can	Biscuits-soda	1	box
Biscuits	1	pkg.	Biscuits--K-Ration			Coffee-ground-8 oz.	1	bag
Eggs-Dry	1	can	Nescafe Coffee-4 oz.	1	can	Jam	1	can
Oatmeal	1	can	Jam or Orange Pres.	1	can	Prunes-8 oz.	1	box
Cocoa	1	can	Prunes or Raisins	1	can	Raisins-8 oz.	1	box
Tea-2 oz.	1	box	Sugar-8oz.	1	box	Sugar-8 oz.	1	bag
Dried Fruit or Pudding	1	can	Chocolate-4oz.	2	bars	Chocolate-5 oz.	1	bar
Sugar-4 oz.	1	box	Soap	2	bars	Soap	1	bar
Chocolate	1	bar	Cigarettes	5	pks.			
Soap	1	bar						

REICH ISSUE

WEEKLY RATION

Army Bread-1 loaf	2100 grams	Soup-Oatmeal, Barley or Pea		3 times
Vegetables-Potatoes	400 grams	Cheese		46 grams
Other Seasonal	?	Sugar		175 grams
Jam	175 grams	Mare		215 grams
Meat		Salt		
Flour---on occasion				

Dear Mother & Father,   Oct. 17, 1944

    Yesterday my first mail from you folks at home arrived. Bill Waters' Long Letter of Aug. 22, and your sequal to it of Aug. 28 brought The news of Laura's Long illness and its inevitable outcome. Being so Totally unprepared for such news you may well imagine the grief and shock with which I received it. Today I have been able To attend church services and consequently feel a bit better. As Father says, "We still have our Faith." More & more do I realize the value of being able to turn to that for assistance at such times as These. I cannot be anything but proud when I think of you folks carrying on as you are. Yours is the greater part of the burden, — not only of This, but of the war and everything that goes with such conditions. We here have become immune to civilian standards of

death and sorrow. It's not a pleasant Thought To realize. Neither is it pleasant To feel of so little comfort and aid to you. I'm glad Ed and Bill could be There. Laura was young, but she has had a full life, and a good life. I know she would rather have it This way then to continue her losing fight. We shall miss her always, but That gives us the additional resolve to carry on for her. My love to you all, Bill

84

Kriegsgefangenenlager (Prisoner-of-war camp)

Datum: Aug 24, 1944

Dear Folks, Everything here is going fine with me. It is very hot at present, but the nights are cool. And fall is not far away. Still have had no news from you at home but am beginning now to Look for my first mail. It should come pretty soon. Hope you are all well. Would like to see you. Love to all, Bill 63

Kriegsgefangenenlager (Prisoner-of-war camp)

Datum: Oct. 29, 1944

Dear Folks, My first parcel came several days ago. It was one of the best first parcels I've seen. Everything was useful and many of the contents were especially so. Highlights were the can opener, dish cloth, Jello, Tooth brushes and powder, soup Tablets, vitamin pills, scissors, and clothes. Keep it up. I have thirteen letters from home now. Love to All, Bill

LIVING THE GOOD LIFE

AFTER A WONDERFUL LEAVE in Orange over Thanksgiving, Frank Jr. drove the Hudson automobile he shared with Tink down to Atlantic City, New Jersey and reported for duty as ordered on December 9, 1944. Lo-and-behold, he was assigned to live at the Ritz-Carlton Hotel on the Boardwalk there as the Air Corps was trying "to provide for our Returnee Officers every service and facility possible so that their stay here will be beneficial and pleasant." Dad's was most pleasant indeed! Meals he mentioned included steaks, lobster, and turkey. There was a game room for returning officers on the third floor, and there were dances on Thursday and Saturday nights. His total personal bill for his week at the Ritz came to just $2.75 (see attachment).

But what were his duties? There were really none. All Air Corps personnel upon return from combat were sent to Atlantic City for rehabilitation. They were given complete physicals and a psychiatric screening and were evaluated for future assignment. As a result of the screening, some pilots were grounded, but Frank was deemed still fit to fly. And on December 16, one week after he'd arrived there, he was granted another leave—this one a twenty-one-day "sick" leave—so he could be home for Christmas. They surely were doing all they could to take care of their combat veterans.

He was back in Atlantic City briefly starting January 6, 1945, and one day while walking on the Boardwalk, he ran into his old Orange Peals buddy Stanley "Bijah" Hinds who asked if he'd like to meet New York Yankee great, Joe DiMaggio. It seems Bijah was staying in the same hotel and on the same floor just two doors down from Joe D. All three were just back from England and combat. Frank said yes, and the next day Bijah introduced Dad to Joe. The three of them had a nice talk. According to Dad, Joe was "a really nice guy."

On January 15, Frank Jr. moved up the road a piece to Mitchell Field where he received orders to report to Hillsgrove Air Field in Rhode Island. He reported there on January 19 and began to log some flight time on the P-47-D, a new high-altitude fighter sporting six machine guns and a shell-firing cannon with the capability of flying at 400 mph on the level and diving at up to 725 mph. Frank logged 18.5 hours on that great plane before the base was closed, and Frank was transferred to Bradley Field in Connecticut on February 14. This was a move he welcomed, and he would remain there until he was sent to Fort Devens, Massachusetts for separation processing and discharge on August 3, 1945.

His initial assignment at Bradley was as a flight instructor for young, inexperienced pilots waiting to go to Europe as replacements. But with the war there rapidly winding down, the training of these young pilots in combat techniques was no longer necessary, and the training was discontinued. Frank was then given the title of Assistant Base Operations Officer.

In reality, he didn't have much to do except take his plane up for a ride on sunny days when the mood struck him. He reported sightseeing jaunts over Mount Monadnock, Lake Sunapee, and the Quabbin Reservoir. But he clearly was often drawn to Orange, and when he went there couldn't resist "buzzing" the house on South Main St. or Henry and Harry's cottage at Lake Mattawa.

One day, he decided to buzz his old friend Bob Harris' gas station on East Main St. He came in particularly low and was having such a good time watching the excitement he was causing at the station he nearly hit the smokestack at the Rodney Hunt Machine Company.

Frank also had much time off, and Orange was less than an hour and a half up the road from Bradley Field. So he was back there often and happened to be there on the afternoon of May 8 when all the church bells in town began ringing wildly. The war in Europe was over! V-E Day!

Everyone was celebrating, and Bob Harris decided spontaneously to have a party at his house. All his old Peals buddies were invited, including Frank and Brud Witty. Frank needed a date, and Brud, who was teaching at Orange High School at the time, fixed him up with a new English teacher there—a dark-haired lass from Maine and Radcliffe College named Barbara Bailey. The party was great, and the date was a smashing success. It would not be their only one.

THE MARCH & MOOSBURG

SATURDAY, JANUARY 27, 1945 was a snowy and very cold day at Stalag Luft III in Sagan, Germany. The POWs there were hoping to be liberated any day by the Russian forces who were just thirty kilometers away. Most prisoners felt it would be impossible for the Germans to try and move them at that point, but all had prepared for that eventuality as best they could, anyway. Layers of clothing, good outerwear, changes of socks, good shoes or boots soaked in margarine to provide some waterproofing, and packets of food were essential.

At 9:30 that evening, the order came down to the 2000 POWs of the South Compound to be ready to move out within the hour. The temperature was below zero, and the snow was deep. But by 11:00, they were on their way out of Sagan headed west. Their German guards had chambered rounds in their rifles, and a rumor came down that they would shoot two prisoners for every one who escaped. The POWs were marched for five hours before stopping on an autobahn overpass at 4:00 AM. With an icy wind howling, they were given a ration of bread and margarine before resuming the march. They pushed on for the balance of the night and until noon on Sunday, taking only a ten-minute rest period each hour. Around noon, they arrived in a town called Grosselton after struggling through deep snow for thirty kilometers while hauling heavy packs. They were understandably completely exhausted and allowed to sleep and rest in unheated barns on whatever straw they could find.

By 6:00 PM, they were off again, marching another twenty-six kilometers that night, too, with many men dropping in the snow from exhaustion. The fallen were loaded into wagons and transported into the next town—Maskau. In Maskau, everyone was quartered in a deserted factory where they stayed for a full twenty-four hours. The only food issued was a smaller portion of bread and margarine. But at least they had access to cold water to refill their canteens. From Maskau they walked twelve kilometers to Graustein and then on to Spremberg. There they were given a cup of barley soup before being loaded into forty-eight boxcars, fifty men to a car. The cars were then locked, and the train pulled out at 7:00 Wednesday evening. It would be a full forty-eight hours before the doors were finally unlocked outside of Regensberg, and the prisoners were allowed out of the boxcars to get fresh air and relieve themselves.

Meanwhile, it was brutally cold inside; there wasn't enough room to lie down; no food was issued; and a number of men were sick. The train carried them through Regensberg and eventually to Moosburg. They arrived there late Friday evening, February 2 and were shunted to a siding where they were left locked in for a third straight night. All night long, men pounded on the doors, pleading for water or just to get out of the filthy, smelly cars for a few minutes of relief. Finally, at 8:00 Saturday morning, they were let out and marched to the POW camp along the siding—Stalag Luft VII A in Moosburg, Bavaria about forty kilometers north of Munich.

How did Lt. William Waters fare on this awful journey? Well, understandably there were no letters written home during this time, and those he wrote later from Moosburg made no mention of the march. But that was his style. Don't worry about me; I'm fine and my life is good. Though he was young, healthy, and strong, he must have been cold, hungry, and miserable for that entire week.

Things were no better at Moosburg, where Tink and the others would be confined for the balance of the war. Initially, the lieutenants were confined to stables where they slept on straw on the floor. They got their first showers in two weeks and were deloused afterward. But their accommodations were still dirty, smelly, and lice filled. The men awoke every morning with dozens of red welts from insect bites. Food was scarce. Because Red Cross parcels had temporarily run out, their diet consisted of two types of dehydrated soup, called Green Death by the POWs, with bread, a little margarine, and an occasional slice of blood sausage.

Tink got two postcards sent home from Moosburg, and, as usual, they told a different story. The first, written February 27, said in part, "Last mail from you came in January. Hope to get more soon, and also a parcel or two. Need toothpowder and a brush, but everything else you send should be food. Much warmer here. Am in best of health. Hope to see you soon. Love, Bill."

The second, written March 27, said, "March nearly over now, so we are all looking forward to spring. We've had some beautiful weather already. The Red Cross is sending food in here from Switzerland via truck convoys, so we are all set in that respect again. Seems good to have a full stomach again. Still anxious to get home and have high hopes of making it before too long."

As March turned to April, Allied planes were everywhere, and the war news was good. Allied artillery could be heard in the distance, and every day it got closer. On the night of April 28, the Germans pulled out, leaving only a small force to guard the camp. On Sunday morning, April 29, a skirmish could be heard just outside the camp. At 12:40 PM the American flag flew over the town of Moosburg. Shortly after that, American tanks rolled into the camp. Tink and his mates were no longer POWS.

THE WAITING GAME

LT. WILLIAM WATERS WAS one of the 27,000 POWs liberated at Moosburg on April 29, 1945 by the United States 14th Armored Division after a brief skirmish with the prison guards. Once freed, the prisoners to a man longed to get home as soon as humanly possible. But they unfortunately learned it was going to take time.

The first challenge was to get the men out of Germany, and since the Nazis didn't surrender until May 8, the logistics of getting transport planes into and out of the Moosburg area had to be carefully considered. Most of the former prisoners remained in the camp for another ten days or so before being airlifted to Le Havre and Camp Lucky Strike in France. Tink caught his flight on May 9, exactly one year and one day after being shot down and captured by the Germans.

About one week before liberation, Tink ran into Lt. Vernon Jackson, a downed B-24 bomber pilot and fellow Orangeite he knew well, by chance at the communal latrine in the middle of the Moosburg camp. The two were overjoyed to see each other and spent the next two weeks bunking together, cooking and eating together, and talking about home. A quote from Jackson about their time together while waiting for flights out appeared in the Orange *Enterprise and Journal* on June 7.

Jackson said, "We had nothing to do but lie around and think about home and food and what might eventually happen to us."

Once the POWs made it to France, there was more waiting to be done. But, as usual, Tink was accepting and philosophical about his situation. In a letter home written Saturday May 12 and received by his mom and dad on the 26th, he had this to say. "I am writing this from Camp Lucky Strike in France. It sure seems good to be over here too. We are being processed, dieted, and generally conditioned for a return to civilization. Even though this is a slow process and has the maddening goal of being at home shortly to make it even more tantalizing, we are all extremely patient and surprisingly acquiescent to everything. Prison life with its barbed wire, privations, and Nazi overlords makes this place a virtual heaven for us all. We're simply basking in the bliss of good old US Army routine, red tape, and G.I. food. I'm sorry that I can't rouse more uneasiness in myself to leave this place. I guess we have instilled in us now a deep reluctance to lose anything that is good even though it promises better returns in the future. Too many of our promises have not panned out."

To me, this paragraph from a letter written seventy-nine years ago said it all. It is eloquent, somewhat sad, and totally heartfelt.

Tink went on to say it might be several more weeks until he got home. He knew he would be sent by boat from Le Havre to the states with the crossing taking about six days. Then, he would be sent to Fort Devens in Massachusetts, where after a couple more days of processing, he would be granted a sixty day leave which he planned to spend in Orange.

"Boy, what a prospect—the whole summer at home."

Finally, he speculated what might happen after his leave. "My hand (left) is pretty good now. Whether it will get me a discharge or not, I don't know. I do think I will have to be hospitalized and undergo treatment for a while after my leave. I hope so because that will mean they can fix it up better than it is now. As it is, I can use it pretty well. Baseball, bowling, etc. are definitely not for me, but fishing, driving, and the like are things I can do. I think I can manage golf too."

It all played out pretty much as Tink thought and hoped. He left France before the end of May, arrived in the states, passed through Fort Devens, and got home to Orange to begin his sixty-day leave on Tuesday, June 5.

In its June 7 edition, the *Enterprise and Journal* reported his arrival thusly: "Lt. William Waters fitted into his comfortable bed at the Waters home on South Main St. Tuesday night as naturally as though it were not something new in his routine. It's been quite a spell since the popular Orange officer has nestled into the sheets at the home of his dad and mother, Dr. and Mrs. Frank T. Waters, and during that period sleeping conditions for him have not always been too satisfactory."

Tink thoroughly enjoyed his time at home and reported back to Fort Devens in early August. There, he underwent a complete medical examination. Further treatment and surgery on his left hand, primarily to remove the remaining shrapnel, was prescribed and accomplished. Best of all, he was deemed unfit to fly due to the condition of his hand, and an immediate discharge was recommended and approved. Tink was sent back home to recuperate around September 1, and his honorable discharge was officially issued November 8, 1945. The war was now officially over for the Waters brothers.

THE POSTWAR
YEARS—FRANK JR. & TINK

By EARLY SUMMER 1945, the two younger Waters brothers, Frank Jr. and Tink, were back at home in Orange enjoying their mother's cooking and laundry service. Awaiting their discharges from the Army Air Corps, they thought about their futures.

Tink, perhaps because he'd had too many idle hours already as a POW, seemed to know exactly what he wanted to do. His first step would be to get his college degree, and he made arrangements to return to Wesleyan University for the fall semester in 1945 where he was an economics major. He figured if he took heavy course loads for both semesters of the 1945-46 academic year, he could finish his degree requirements during the summer 1946 session.

Almost twenty-five, he also seemed ready to find the right girl and settle down. As we've seen, he had several brief flings during his pilot training, and he also had a bevy of Orange girls who wrote to him regularly. But there was only one girl who stayed the course through the long year when he was a POW and out of commission. The blond, blue-eyed, and freckled Orange lass, Geraldine McKenna, never stopped writing him or reaching out to his parents. She even dropped off a gift for him at Christmastime 1944. Tink and Gerry had dated a few times casually before he went off to war, and they quickly reconnected when he got back home. By the fall of 1945, they were dating steadily and getting serious.

Frank Jr. was less certain of his course forward both in terms of school or work and his love life. Two years older than Tink, and never an enthusiastic student, he wasn't at all sure he wanted to return to college. So he secured a job at the local post office and signed on to a part-time job as an assistant basketball coach at Orange High. As we know, he had been somewhat smitten with dark-haired English teacher, Barbara Bailey, on their V-E Day date, and they dated a few more times over the next month or so. But school let out, and Barb went home to Maine for the summer before things got serious.

Frank drifted along, playing the field that summer, just happy to be home. On Labor Day, September 1, 1945, Barbara returned to town for the new school year. As she walked along South Main St., carrying her suitcase and headed from the train station to Mrs. Burrill's rooming house, a car pulled up alongside her and a man asked, "Would you like a ride, Ma'am?"

The man was Frank, and it is unknown whether his taxi service was pure coincidence, but it was definitely fortuitous for both of them. They picked up where they left off in June, enjoyed many good and fun-filled evenings with Tink and Gerry, and by late fall were every bit as serious as the other couple.

About that time, both Tink and Barbara began working on Frank to return to Wesleyan for his degree, too. He finally agreed to go back in January 1946 but not to take economics courses. He switched his major to geology, affectionately called rocks for jocks by more serious students, and supplemented his geology course load with various religion and philosophy courses guaranteed not to be too taxing. He enlisted Barbara's aid in writing papers for him and was reportedly pleased when they got an A on a religion paper. It was believed to be the first A of his life.

As an aside some twenty years later, I, too, leaned on Barbara to write Wesleyan college papers for me. I believe her finest effort on my behalf was entitled "Emily Dickinson as an Epigrammatic Walt Whitman." I got an A+ and to this day have no idea what the title even means.

The 1945-46 academic year passed quickly and according to plan. Tink took the courses and load he needed to stay on track; Frank got a successful semester in. Both grew closer to their girls. Come spring, Tink asked Gerry to marry him, and their engagement was announced in local papers on June 20. No date was set for the wedding, but Tink had a schedule to keep.

The ceremony took place at the Central Congregational Church in Orange on Saturday, September 28, 1946 at 3:00 in the afternoon. His brother, Frank, was Bill's best man, while Gerry's sister, Althea, was the maid of honor. The reception was also in the church, and afterward the newlyweds left by automobile for a honeymoon in Canada. On return, Tink, who had completed his bachelor's degree requirements during the 1946 summer session at Wesleyan, would begin a job in Washington, DC with the Civil Aeronautics Board.

As for Frank, he dilly-dallied a bit but convinced Barbara to stay in Orange that summer where she got a job as a hostess at a local restaurant.

On the evening of August 18, he said to her, "I'll be up to get you at 10:00 tomorrow morning and we'll go get you a ring."

There was no bended knee or even an inquiry about whether she wanted to get married. That was just his style. Afterward, they came home to 185 South Main to tell Grandma Waters and show her the ring.

Purportedly she cried and said, "I'll be glad to have someone else wash your shirts."

With Barbara's help, Frank returned to Wesleyan in the fall of 1946 and by spring had secured enough credits to graduate. In the fall of '46, his old soccer coach, Hugh McCurdy, harassed him to rejoin the soccer team. Older, out of shape, and a heavy smoker, he resisted for a while but finally acquiesced. His first game, and the last, was at Worcester Tech. Somehow, he managed to score not one or two but five goals in the first half! But early in the second half he fell awkwardly and broke his wrist. And that was it for the game, the season, and his soccer career.

Frank and Barbara were married June 28, 1947 at St. Mark's Methodist Church in Brookline, Massachusetts. Returning the favor, Tink was his brother's best man while Barbara's sister, Lois, was her maid of honor. The reception was at Edwin and Margie's house in Wakefield where the guests dined on lobster rolls and beer. One notable couple in attendance was John Stearns and his new bride, Lucy Standish.

Always a romantic, Frank spent weeks planning an exquisite honeymoon sure to wow his new bride. First, they spent two nights at Lake Winnipesaukee and took a leisurely drive through the White Mountains on the middle day. Then, they headed south to Boston, Barbara's favorite city, where they enjoyed nice dinners, spent time with Barb's aunts, Nell and Edna, and most importantly attended Red Sox baseball games at Fenway Park four afternoons in a row, allowing Barbara to get to know intimately Bobby Doerr, Ted Williams, and Dom DiMaggio and perhaps to wonder, "What have I gotten myself into?"

Tink and Gerry spent the better part of a year in Washington, DC, but he didn't love his job with the Civil Aeronautics Board. They both missed New England. So in the summer of 1947, Tink joined Aetna Life and Casualty in its home office in Hartford, Connecticut, and they moved to West Hartford. A few weeks later, their first child, a little girl they named Laura Gay after Tink's late sister, was born on August 29, 1947. About two and a half years later a second daughter, Nancy Jean, was born on February 12, 1950. Meanwhile, Tink was steadily moving up the ladder in the Group Claims department at Aetna.

After his wedding and Wesleyan graduation, Frank joined his new bride on the faculty at Orange High School for the 1947-48 school year. He taught physical education and coached football, basketball, and baseball. He and Barbara arranged to rent a second-floor apartment in Lil McKenna's (Gerry's mother) house at 15 West Myrtle St. for the ungodly sum of $12 per month. They spent the fall painting and fixing it up while still residing with his mother and father on South Main St. Over Christmas vacation they moved the couple of hundred yards to their new place.

It had been almost forty years since Edwin's birth, but Frank Sr. and Lue, he 71 and she 69, were finally empty nesters. Those poor people!

Anyway, a few months later Frank Jr. and Barbara welcomed a little boy they named Frank the third on September 13, 1948. Marcia followed February 19, 1950, and John rounded out the family June 14, 1954.

The decade of the forties had not been an easy one for the two younger Waters brothers nor their parents, but their lives were on an upward swing as the new decade commenced.

THE POSTWAR YEARS—THE OTHERS

J EAN WAS A PRETTY woman, a quiet woman, maybe even a shy woman. Her husband, Osh, was good looking, dashing and debonair, and a bit of a ladies' man. She liked to cook, to read, to work on her needlepoint, be around family, and live a low-key lifestyle. He liked a good party and an active social life. He was a good pilot and a leader of men who had steadily climbed through the ranks of the Army Air Corps during the war years. He was a full colonel at its conclusion, so it was not a big surprise when he decided to stay in the service and make the air corps his career.

Jean and Osh had been married for more than six years at war's end, and they had no children. While Osh had been off fighting the Nazis, Jean had spent the last two years of the war back in Orange around family and making herself useful. But with his assignment now stateside, she joined him at Wright Patterson Air Force Base near Dayton, Ohio where he would be a commanding officer. As such, he (they) hosted dinner parties frequently, and he often worked late into the evening. He may or may not have had a lady friend or two.

It wasn't surprising the marriage began to show signs of stress and conflict. For a while, they hung together and tried to make things work. After all, they had been together since high school. But Jean became more and more miserable. Eventually, late in 1950 she packed up her car and left, driving non-stop to Connecticut and showing up on Tink's doorstep.

He and Gerry were wonderful, taking her in and finding her a job and a place to live and guiding her through divorce proceedings. It wasn't a pleasant divorce, and Jean was a mess. She was severely depressed, and Tink and Gerry got her help and counseling with their minister, Wallace Fisk, at the West Hartford Universalist Church. Ironically, Reverend Fisk was from Orange and was well known to the Waters family.

Over time, Jean righted her ship, developed a circle of friends at the Aetna where she worked, and bought a house on Webster Hill Blvd. in West Hartford. She also developed a penchant for convertibles and every three years treated herself to the latest model Chevy Bel Air. It was a long time before she was ready to date seriously though.

John Stearns found himself a widower in his mid-thirties with young sons aged ten and nine to raise by himself. He was understandably lonely and stressed. But within a year of Laura's passing, a friend introduced him to a widow of similar age and station, Lucy Standish. She had lost her husband in 1943, leaving her with a three-year-old son and a seven-week-old daughter. Two years later she was living in Wethersfield with her children and was as lonely and stressed as he was. John and Lucy hit it off immediately and married in June 1946. They raised their blended family in the Walden St. home in West Hartford, and together they did a wonderful job of parenting. With three active boys and one shy little girl, that was no small task. But Lucy and John provided much love, and she, in particular, was a strict disciplinarian while he was a good provider. To their credit, they encouraged young John and David to remain close to the Waters family.

John Jr. and David had strong bonds to their grandparents, Frank and Lue, their uncles, Frank Jr. and Tink, and especially to their Aunt Jean who had cared for them when their mother was sick. And their feelings were reciprocated.

In nearly every letter written during their military years, Frank Jr. and Tink asked about or remembered their nephews. In August

1943, Frank sent the boys a 50-caliber machine-gun bullet, two clips of 30 caliber ammo, and a small parachute used with a flare.

In a letter Tink wrote May 12, 1945, letting his folks know he was no longer a POW and would soon be home, he didn't forget the boys either. "Got a couple of Kraut winter hats I'm bringing for Johnny and Dave."

Not surprisingly, in those postwar years, Johnny and Dave were a popular presence in Orange and at other Waters' gatherings large and small. With much love all around them, both boys grew up to be strong and successful men, and their devoted uncles, aunts, and especially their Waters grandparents benefitted mightily by having John and David in their lives.

For Edwin and Margie and their daughter, Sally, and dog, Wendy, life was good in the aftermath of World War II. Ed enjoyed his job as a research chemist with Monsanto Chemical Co. in Everett, Massachusetts, and he dabbled in politics in his adopted hometown of Wakefield, Massachusetts. He soon became chairman of the republican town committee there. In November 1946 Ed and Margie welcomed a son, Edwin Stone Waters Jr. to their household at 22 White Circle.

With a nice home, a good job, a little girl and a little boy, the requisite family dog, and large and supportive families behind them, they were living the dream returning servicemen and young couples across America aspired to in the late 40s. And then disaster struck. On December 15, 1948, Ed suffered a brain aneurism and died at age forty, leaving behind a four-year-old daughter, a two-year-old son, and a grief-stricken wife.

How could this happen? And why? There were, of course, no definitive answers. When Edwin was in high school, he had been standing and riding in the back of a pickup truck and was knocked unconscious when he struck his head on a bridge overpass the vehicle passed under. He was unconscious for two days but seemingly made a complete recovery with no lingering side effects. Could this accident have caused this aneurism twenty-some years later? We'll never know. But Margie somehow regrouped and soldiered on. She obtained a license and opened a daycare business in her home. She raised her children, Sally and Stoney, by herself, and she did a very fine job.

Lastly, when the war finally ended, Frank Sr. and Lue breathed a sigh of relief. They had buried a daughter, but their two youngest sons and a son-in-law, air corps pilots all, somehow managed to get back home in one piece. They were blessed with two wonderful grandsons and a beautiful granddaughter who were growing bigger by the day.

Their lives returned to normal in those years of 1946-48, but much was happening around their family. Thankfully, much of the news was good. Tink and Frank Jr. found girls, got engaged, and soon were married. Frank Sr. and Lue were delighted with and strongly approved of their new daughters-in-law. From Lue's perspective, she was happy to have someone else take care of her then late-twenties sons. Then the babies came fast and furious. Stoney was born to Ed and Margie in November 1946; Laura was born to Tink and Gerry on August 29, 1947; Waddy arrived September 13, 1948; and Nancy and Marcia came along in February 1950. There was never a dull moment for Pop and Lue.

Meanwhile, though he turned 70 in 1946, Frank Sr. continued to practice dentistry and chair the Orange School Committee while Lue served a term.as president of the Orange Women's Club. These times were good, but there was more hardship to come for the heads of the Waters' family who had already borne so much.

No parents should ever have to lose one child yet alone two. But in December 1948, that was exactly what Frank and Lue had to face when their eldest, 40-year-old Edwin, died suddenly, leaving behind a spouse and two young children. At the same time, their daughter, Jeannette, was growing more miserable as her marriage fell apart.

Through it all, these two septuagenarians found a reservoir of resolve not only to keep going but also to serve as a rock for the children and grandchildren around them to lean on and cling to.

In the spring of 1951, when I was almost three, I was walking along South Main St. near Witty's Funeral Home with my mom. I was atop a foot-high stone wall when I fell, breaking my upper central incisor. I was quickly taken to my grandfather's dental office where he made repairs by providing me with a solid gold cap, which I absolutely loved for the next two years until that baby tooth fell out. This was one of the last dental surgeries Dr. Frank T. Waters performed. In June 1951, he suffered a massive heart attack. And though he recovered sufficiently to return home at the end of the month, in the middle of the night on July 2, 1951, he got out of bed, went to the bathroom, returned to his bed, turned on his side and pulled his knees up into his favorite sleeping position, and passed away. He was a few months short of his 75th birthday.

After his death, Frank Jr., Barbara, and their kids moved into the house at 185 South Main St. to be with Lue. She graciously adjusted to this new arrangement and divided her time between Orange and West Hartford where she would stay with Jean and be near Tink and his family.

I have fond memories of creeping into her bed early in the morning and having her read *Grimm's Fairy Tales* to me. She was a wonderful lady.

Lue had a heart attack early in 1957 and died in August that year.

JULY 1962

It was a perfect summer Saturday at the south end of Lake Mattawa in Orange, Massachusetts. The sun was shining, the breezes were light, and the temperature was in the low eighties. The happy sounds of children playing in the water wafted through the air. Four adults sat in Adirondack chairs on the lawn between two cottages, sipping drinks.

The cottage on the left, looking out at the lake, belonged to Frank Waters Jr. and his wife, Barbara; the one on the right was owned by William "Tink" Waters and his wife, Gerry. The Waters brothers, so close all their lives, were back together again, and this spot on the lake in the town they grew up in was their favorite place on earth.

Frank and Barbara lived in Orange in the house he'd grown up in at 185 South Main St. They had three children: Frank the third or "Waddy," almost fourteen, Marcia age twelve, and John David age eight. After a dozen years teaching and coaching, Frank then worked as the personnel manager at the Minute Tapioca/Minute Rice plant in town. Barbara had returned to teaching two years earlier when John reached school age.

Tink was a rising executive in the Group Department at Aetna Life and Casualty in Hartford and lived in West Hartford with Gerry and their two daughters: Laura (Lolly), who was almost fifteen and Nancy, who was twelve and exactly one week older than her cousin Marcia.

On that weekend, and many others through the summer months, Frank and Tink's older sister, Jean, was with them there at the lake.

A decade after being divorced from Osh, Jean also lived in West Hartford and worked at the Aetna in a job Tink had gotten her. Aunt Jean was a welcome weekend presence at the lake. She doted on her nieces and nephews, always brought an array of goodies, and didn't need to be entertained.

Occasionally, Jean brought her late sister's son, David, who also lived and worked in the Hartford area, with her for a weekend with family. Jean and David had developed a lifetime bond in that awful, long ago summer of '44 when Jean ran the Stearns household and cared for John and David as their mom and her sister unsuccessfully battled leukemia.

These summer weekends in the sixties had a regular rhythm and pace to them. The weekend began like clockwork on Friday afternoon between 5:30-5:45 when Tink arrived from Hartford, always with a wave and a toot of his horn as he rounded the corner of the dirt road leading to the cottages. Within minutes, Tink was in a bathing suit, and Tink and Gerry and Frank and Barb had drinks in their hands, settled either around Frank and Barb's circle of lawn chairs or on Tink and Gerry's patio overlooking the lake. More often than not, each family did their own thing at mealtime, but combined cookouts or big outdoor Sunday breakfasts were not uncommon.

Tink had a variety of interests. He enjoyed fishing either for trout in the morning or horned pout at night; he had a regular tennis group at Deckie Wood's court at the north end of the lake; and he enjoyed a game of golf.

His brother's idea, however, of a great weekend was to have a work project to do—the bigger the better. He'd do them alone but preferred to get anyone who was around involved—especially his brother.

I'm quite sure Tink didn't love it as my father did, but he was a good sport, and they did good work in tandem. Together, using railroad ties, lots of rocks and gravel, and much backbreaking effort, they created retaining walls and shore-side seating areas in front of both cottages. They also built Tink a bunkhouse/woodshed and painted each other's cottages. Frank's fall back project, accomplished over ten-fifteen years, was putting a full basement under his cottage. All excavation was with pail and shovel, all footings and flooring were with mortar mixed by hand, and every concrete block for the walls was placed and set by him—a self-taught skill. He did it all, though I mixed plenty of batches of mortar using a shovel, buckets, and a hoe. My cousin, Stoney, and I were often paid $2.00 each for filling Dad's trailer with dirt from the cellar hole one pail at a time.

But I digress. Saturday was usually bridge night for the grown-ups. The teams were always the same—Tink & Barb vs. Frank & Gerry. This was no relaxed, social card game. Scores and running standings were kept on a scoreboard that eventually spanned nearly two decades. Sundays were largely spent around the waterfront with Dad often directing games and watersports for us kids. Unless it was raining, Sunday dinner was always at the picnic table. Very early Monday morning Tink headed back to Hartford. Jean usually left after dinner on Sunday.

One Saturday afternoon, Marcia, Nancy, and John were swimming on the waterfront while Lol and Aunt Jean got some sun on the dock. Frank and Tink had taken a beer break, and Barb and Gerry had joined them in the circle of chairs between the camps. I was shooting baskets on my new clay basketball court (another recent Frank project) behind the bunkhouse near the driveway.

As I was shooting, a car with out-of-state plates pulled tentatively in.

A man in his forties got out and said to me, "I'm looking for Frank Waters."

I replied, "That's my dad. I'll go get him."

I called my father over, and the man introduced himself. "I served in the same bomber group as your brother, Bill, and I always remembered he was from Orange, Massachusetts and had a brother Frank who was also a pilot. My wife and I were on Rte. 2 headed for Maine, and when I saw the sign for Orange decided to stop and see if I could find you just to say hello and tell you how much I thought of your brother."

My dad then said, "Well, get your wife and come on over and tell him yourself."

The man was shocked and stammered. "He's here? He's alive? His plane was shot down, and he was MIA. I thought he was dead."

"No, he got out and was in a POW camp for the rest of the war," Dad said. He turned and shouted across the lawn. "William, come over here."

I had tears in my eyes as I watched these two former mates embrace, and I hung close as the six adults talked and reminisced. Dad and Tink almost never talked about their WW II years, but that afternoon I heard a lot and learned a lot about their combat experiences—particularly Tink's harrowing journey.

WATERS FAMILY REUNION
1991

LABOR DAY WEEKEND AT Lake Mattawa can sometimes be quite fallish. The sun is lower in the sky, shadows are longer, temperatures are often in the low seventies. If the prevailing north to south wind is brisk rolling down the lake toward the Waters' cottages at the south end, swimming and other summer activities aren't very appealing.

Fortunately, Saturday, August 31, 1991 provided lots of sun, temps in the low eighties, and gentle breezes. It was a perfect summer's day for the reunion held there. The reunion idea had been hatched back in 1987, and this would be the fifth annual and the third held at the Lake Mattawa site that held such fond memories for all family members. This 1991 gathering would be the biggest and best ever.

From the Frank T. Waters tree, matriarch Jeannette (77) and patriarchs Frank Jr. (73) and Tink (71) were not only present but actively engaged and in their glory. That year, their generation was also represented by Sally and Ralph Fisher and Pat Cousins Waters (widow of Cousin Bill) from the Lewis Waters branch. And every one of Frank and Lue's grandchildren were there with spouses and children in tow: John and David Stearns, Sally and Stoney Waters (Edwin's children), Waddy, Marcia, and John Waters (Frank's and Barbara's kids), and Laura and Nancy Waters (Tink's and Gerry's offspring). Pat Waters had all four of her children (Jiffy, Candy, Billy, and David) and their families with her, and Sally and Ralph had two of their sons and several grandchildren along as well.

In total, attendance exceeded eighty. It was the first time in at least thirty years this many Waters relatives had been together in a social setting. It was a dream come true for Jean, Frank, and Tink and I'm quite sure for Sally and Pat too.

For activities there were games aplenty to be played, but the burning questions of the day were whether Frank Jr. and Tink could defend their croquet championship won the summer before at the 1990 reunion held at the Stearns' estate in the mountains of Vermont (they did), and whether the egg toss would be played fairly this year unlike the one two years earlier when Frank Jr. slipped a hard-boiled egg into the contest, which wasn't discovered until seven-year-old Tyler Waters shockingly was part of the victorious duo. Alas, it wasn't—Frank did it again.

On that warm day, there was also lots of swimming. It was always a treat to see David Stearns and his sister-in-law, Judy, very strong swimmers both, glide so effortlessly through the water. That afternoon, though both were close to sixty, they organized a swim across the lake (about three-quarters of a mile) and were joined by a gang of about twenty, including young adults, teenagers, and at least one twelve-year-old (Waddy's daughter, Jody). Two boats accompanied the swimmers. Nearly everyone made it all the way, and it was great fun to watch the teamwork and camaraderie of these determined Waters swimmers of all ages.

Through the afternoon, Jean held court in the circle of chairs on the lawn with a stream of eager listeners stopping by. Then, just prior to dinner, all attendees gathered there for a Waters trivia contest. Favorite questions included when did the first Waters (Samuel) arrive in America from England? (Answer: 1859.) What was Samuel's wife's full maiden name? (Answer: Mary Weeks Baldock.) What town in England were they from? (Answer: Wadhurst.) Name three Waters who have parachuted from an airplane. (Answer: Tink, Sally, and Stoney.) And what was Grandpa Waters' favorite song to sing while washing up before supper? (Answer: "On the Road to Mandalay.")

Then, it was time to eat—the usual picnic fare of burgers and dogs, corn on the cob, and assorted salads. But no Waters cookout is complete without home-baked beans. That year, Frank Jr., who had to make everything a competition, challenged Tink to a contest to see who could make the best pot of beans. The voting was close, but when the tally was in, Tink won. Frank was crushed—even more so when it was revealed Tink's were actually doctored canned beans and not the made from scratch batch Frank had edicted.

As the sun set behind the hills on the west side of the lake, the attendees, especially those with younger children, packed their things. But Jean and Frank and Tink, weary though they must have been, seemed to linger in their chairs, unwilling to see the great day end.

I think Frank and Tink, especially, were pleased to have their children, grandchildren, and extended family around them on those Lake Mattawa grounds that had been their happy place for many, many years. I like to think those kids and grandkids and the cottages might have caused them to think the incredible sacrifices they made for their country and their family some fifty years earlier had been for a good and worthwhile cause.

EPILOGUE

MY FATHER, FRANK JR., requested a drumstick for his Thanksgiving dinner when he returned from combat in 1944. His mother and father made sure he got one. When he had a family of his own, he would stand at the head of the Thanksgiving dinner table each holiday and carve that year's bird to order with a carving knife he'd spent much of the morning sharpening. All who were present knew without a word being said that one of the drumsticks was earmarked for him. And no one had a problem with that. His sacrifice, hardship, and service to his country in those World War II years had earned him a lifetime right to the part of the turkey he liked best.

They are all gone now—have been for quite a while. Tink was the first to go in the early spring of 1993, while Frank passed in December 2003. Jean hung on until August 2008 shortly after her 94th birthday. Since then, we've also lost John and David Stearns and Tink's younger daughter, Nancy. The surviving six of Frank Sr. and Lue's grandchildren are all in our seventies now, save Sally who recently turned eighty, and we are solidly in the front row of all family pictures.

My cousin, Lol, who has been heavily involved in this project with me over these last several months, has asked this question several times. "Did they really not talk about those war years, or did I just not take the time to listen?"

I think the answer is probably somewhere in between. I believe they spoke little about their wartime journeys in those years when we, their children, were growing up and were young adults. But I think they would have told us more if only we had taken the time to pry and to listen, especially when they were older.

I do know I am eternally grateful for the treasure trove of letters, memorabilia, and notations my father left behind, and I am certain Lol feels the same way about Tink's things. Each of us owes a huge debt of gratitude to Pop, Dr. Frank T. Waters, for having the foresight and bulldog determination to keep track of, catalog, and pass along all those wartime family letters and memorabilia.

I have had a great time with this project, and I have learned so much about those war years in general, and my father, Uncle Tink, and other family members in particular. I'm sure I know my father and uncle better now than I ever did when they were alive.

And I have such gratitude for the sacrifices they made so we might be free today and enjoying a good and comfortable life.

REFERENCES

1. Young, D. (1950). Rommel, The Desert Fox. New York, NY, USA: Harper. Retrieved 2025

About the author

A 1970 graduate of Wesleyan University, Middletown, Connecticut, Frank T. Waters III became a published author of a short story titled "The Secret of Bears Den" at ten years old. He regularly amuses himself with writing fantasy football newsletters and Thursday golf reports.

His first "real" literary effort, *A Drumstick for Thanksgiving Please* fulfills a thirty-year-old promise to his father, a World War II fighter pilot. What the future holds for Frank as a writer is not yet determined.

Frank owned a successful insurance agency in West Hartford, Connecticut for almost thirty-five years. From 1997-2016, he coached high school varsity girls' basketball in Avon, Connecticut. His career record boasts 378 wins and 95 losses with one state championship.

Living in Avon, Connecticut with his wife of fifty years, Janet, Frank enjoys his two adult children and three grandchildren and plays a lot of golf. In his thirty-eighth year as a commissioner of a fantasy football league, he continues pursuing sports he has loved since childhood.

www.ingramcontent.com/pod-product-compliance
Lightning Source LLC
Chambersburg PA
CBHW071010120626
46546CB00003B/1020